THE
SOCIOLOGY
OF THE
MASS MEDIA

David Glover

Causeway Books

12503948

British Library Cataloguing in Publication Data

Glover, David
 The sociology of the mass media.—(Themes and
 perspectives in sociology; 1)
 1. Mass media—Social aspects
 I. Title   II. Series
 302.2'34   HM258

 ISBN 0-946183-05-8

Causeway Press Ltd.
PO Box 13, Ormskirk, Lancashire L39 5HP
©Causeway Press Ltd., 1984

1st Impression April 1984

Production by BPMS, Ormskirk.
Typesetting by Bookform, Merseyside
Printed and bound in England by Robert Hartnoll,
Bodmin, Cornwall

Contents

Chapter Three

The Structure and Organization of the Mass Media

Preface

It is a cliché to say that sociology is concerned with the study of society. What this leaves out is that in practice sociologists have mostly been interested in industrial societies: with how they have grown up, how people behave in them, the problems they face and their impact upon the non-industrial world. Indeed, industralism served as a catalyst for the development of sociology as a discipline.

For the majority of readers of this book industralism is a way of life and forms the basis of their judgements about what societies ought to be like. Yet industrial societies are both very new and very different from those that have gone before. One of the things that makes them so different is the existence of the mass media. It is impossible to imagine modern societies without film, television and radio or mass-produced records, books and newspapers. Beginning in the nineteenth century the existing means of communication were revolutionised by the application of industrial techniques from which completely new cultural forms were developed. By 1910 film, radio, photography, telegraphy and the phonograph had all been invented and television was less than a generation away. It is important to remember that the industrial revolution did not just create the steam locomotive and the spinning jenny – it produced the steam driven printing press as well.

Not everyone saw these changes as an unmixed blessing. Karl Marx, writing in 1871, noted that 'the daily press and the telegraph, which in a moment spread inventions over the whole earth, fabricate more myths . . . in one day than could formerly have been done in a century'. As we will see, criticisms of the media have continued unabated down to the present day. A book as short as this can give only a brief indication of the contribution sociologists have made to debates about the mass media. What it does attempt is to offer a taste of sociological work in this area by showing the kinds of questions that have been asked and the perspectives from which sociologists have sought to answer them.

I would like to thank Ros Billington, Jerry Booth and Michael Haralambos for helpful comments on earlier versions of this book, and Molly Jowett for assistance with the typing.

David Glover
January 1984

In memory of
Seth and Hilda Glover
and for
Anne Rogers

Chapter One

Media Effects

The Martians Are Coming

> The girls...huddled around their radios trembling
> and weeping in each other's arms. They separated them-
> selves from their friends only to take their turn at the
> telephone to make long distance calls to their parents,
> saying goodbye for what they thought might be the last
> time... Terror-stricken girls, hoping to escape from the
> Mars invaders, rushed to the basement of the dormitory.
> (Cantril, 1940, p. 53)

With these words an American college student, a victim of one of the
most extraordinary collective delusions ever to have taken place,
recalled her experience of a notorious radio broadcast and the fears it
provoked in her and her family and friends. Over a million people were
frightened or disturbed by Orson Welles' 1938 radio play *War of the
Worlds* which dramatised an H. G. Wells' tale of an invasion from
outer space with such terrifyingly convincing effect that people fled for
their lives. So devastating was its impact that the rules governing broadcasting in the United States were changed to prevent anything like it
from happening again.

This story symbolises much of our thinking about the influence the
media have upon us. Many believe that television or the printed word
can mould individual personalities or completely transform society like
some genie in a magic bottle that has escaped our control. Orson
Welles' power over his audience seems to sum up this feeling of
impotence and it is hardly surprising that the story of the radio invasion
is now deeply lodged in our folk-memories.

How and why so many people came to believe that they really were being invaded by a strange race of creatures armed with heat ray guns and poisonous black gas is a question to which I will return later in this chapter. For the moment I simply want to note that the Welles' broadcast raises in a peculiarly vivid form the whole issue of the media's effects upon us. Like the Martians in the play, the media often appear in public debates as a kind of alien force poised to take over our lives and acting upon us without our being able to resist. Nowadays radio is seldom perceived as a very dangerous medium, but it is worth remembering that the fears which are currently voiced about television or video were once associated with the 'wireless'. The 'invasion from Mars' helps alert us to the fact that anxieties about the media have a history, and that the notion of their having powerful and all-pervasive effects upon us is far from new. To emphasise this point, consider the following:

> One powerful agent for the depraving of the boyish classes of our towns and cities is to be found in the cheap shows and theatres, which are so specially opened and arranged for the attraction and ensnaring of the young . . . it is not to be wondered at that the boy who is led on to haunt them becomes rapidly corrupted and demoralised, and seeks to be the doer of the infamies which have interested him as a spectator. (quoted in Murdock & McCron, 1979, p. 51)

Although the language is old – this passage was written in 1851 – the argument is still around today. Only the media have moved on. Instead of the theatre, our worries now focus upon television or video, though the corruption of the young continues to be a key theme.

What has tended to happen is that the arguments and anxieties associated with the culturally dominant media of the past have been re-directed as new media have come into existence. This pattern is reflected in the history of research into media effects. As we will see in the next section, the earliest mass media research reflected these long-standing fears.

The Hypodermic Syringe Model

The first studies of the mass media were based on the theory that their effects upon our lives were very simple and direct. For example, it was assumed that the mere portrayal of criminality by the media was enough to stimulate a rise in criminal behaviour amongst a vulnerable audience. This perspective came to be known as the 'hypodermic' theory. It saw media effects as like an injection into the veins of the audience, an injection that was usually harmful, though occasionally beneficial. Much of this research was preoccupied with the impact of the cinema, particularly on the young. Most famous of all were the studies financed by the Payne Fund, a body set up in New York in 1928 to look at the relationship between film-watching and the attitudes, emotions and behaviour of young people, especially the phenomenon of juvenile crime. Yet although these studies were very detailed, they were rather inconclusive. It was hard to demonstrate any consistent causal connection between cinema attendance and delinquency, and where links were found they were far from simple and were difficult to explain.

Despite its weaknesses the hypodermic syringe model has been extremely influential. Part of the reason for its appeal lies in the fact that its roots are to be found in ideas that have become deeply ingrained in modern societies. In the first place, the hypodermic model drew upon assumptions about social change that went back at least as far as the nineteenth century and which can be seen in the passage about the corruption of young boys by cheap popular theatres quoted above. It was assumed that the social upheavals associated with industrialisation had made people extremely vulnerable so that they were easily swayed by any attempt to grab their attention or provide them with novel experiences. Thus they were prey to political demagogues and readily duped by the new mass media. The reason for this vulnerability was that industrialisation had broken down the older, more settled communities in which people had a sense of belonging, but had failed to put anything in their place to recreate a feeling of order and identity. Instead society was increasingly becoming a mass of isolated individuals cut adrift from local social ties and with little to channel their energies or hold their desires in check. Hence it was called a 'mass society'. Echoes of this view can be found in social theorists as different as Alexis de Tocqueville and John Stuart Mill, and later Vilfredo Pareto and Karl Mannheim. Similar ideas can also be detected behind Durkheim's concept of anomie, with its notion of appetites and aspirations that are no longer restrained by society. In a mass society in which traditional forms of social control were seen to be breaking down, the mass media appeared as a powerful force controlling behaviour.

A second source of the hypodermic theory derived from the rise of behaviourism in psychology in the early years of this century. This school of thought saw all human action as modelled on the conditioned reflex so that one's personality consisted of nothing more than responses to stimuli in the individual's environment which formed stable and recognisable patterns of behaviour – hence the name 'behaviourism'. It therefore seemed to provide strong grounds for thinking that social action was heavily determined by external forces rather than being a matter of personal choice based upon social beliefs and knowledge. The mass media appeared to be an obvious candidate for any theory of the powerful stimuli to be found in modern society. Behaviourism thus dovetailed neatly with the pessimistic assumptions of the earlier 'mass society' theorists.

The weakness of this way of thinking about the media will be readily apparent. Audiences are assumed to be manipulable and dependent while the mass media's capacity to influence them is seen as enormous, the two being connected together by a relatively simple one-way mechanism of social learning. However the mass media affect us, it is clearly more complex than was ever imagined in the early days of research. Hypodermic theories are rarely found in their pure form today and current work which springs from this tradition has considerably modified the original model by bringing in more subtle social psychological processes of attitude formation, as in the theories of the American researcher Melvin DeFleur. Where this sort of thinking does survive is in public discussions about the media which are often haunted by the ghosts of theories that have long since passed away. There is a certain irony in this for, as two of its critics were quick to point out, the hypodermic theory was partly developed in the first place 'from an image of the potency of the mass media which was in the popular mind' (Katz & Lazarsfeld, 1955, p. 17). The hypodermic syringe model had a very narrow view of the media's audience. People were seen as passive receivers of the media's message. They had little or no say in the matter. They appeared to be overpowered by a mass media which simply injected its message. Yet audiences are made up of people who select and reject, make judgments and communicate with each other. These observations formed an important part of the 'two-step flow model' which will now be examined.

The Two-Step Flow Model

If the hypodermic theory was flawed by an unsophisticated and un-sociological view of the media's audience it was this major defect that its principal challengers set themselves to remedy. This point was emphasised from the very beginning when Elihu Katz and Paul Lazarsfeld gave their path-breaking book *Personal Influence* the sub-title *The Part Played by People in the Flow of Mass Communications*. They altered the whole direction of media research and founded a theoretical tradition which was to dominate media sociology in the post-war period and was still being described as 'the dominant paradigm in the field' as late as 1978 (Gitlin, 1978, p. 207).

The origins of the paradigm go back to a study of the 1940 American presidential election carried out by Paul Lazarsfeld, a German émigré and a former mathematician who had switched to sociology and whose work was to revolutionise the analysis of social survey data. What the election study showed was that the impact of the media upon people's votes was far less than the hypodermic theory would lead one to expect. Only a quarter of the voters made up their minds during the campaign itself, and as many as 50% of all voters had not only decided who to vote for six months before the election, but had maintained their preference right up to polling day. Amongst those who did decide which way to vote during the campaign period it was not the political discussion in the media which influenced them so much as the opinions of what the study called 'molecular leaders', individuals whose views and ideas were respected and important in the voters' immediate social circle. Lazarsfeld believed that this finding warranted further investigation and so the election survey, appropriately entitled *The People's Choice*, was followed up with a study of how opinions were formed in 'a middle-sized American city' in Illinois, the results of which appeared in Katz and Lazarsfeld's *Personal Influence*.

The book confirmed and considerably refined Lazarsfeld's earlier discovery. Far from being an atomised mass of isolated individuals, society was pre-eminently a matter of *group* life (indeed Katz and Lazarsfeld wrote enthusiastically of 'the "rediscovery" of the primary group'), and it was how these groups were organised that counted in the formation of social attitudes. In other words, we are influenced by members of our family, our friends and co-workers and therefore those who direct and help form opinions are not special high status individuals but are found at every level of society. As Katz and Lazarsfeld put it 'opinion leadership is an integral part of the give-and-take of everyday personal relationships' and 'an opinion leader can best be thought of as a group member playing a key communication role' (p. 33).

This seems to leave the mass media out in the cold, almost a complete reversal of the hypodermic theory. However, the media were found to be important, but in a different way than had been previously thought. It was the opinion leaders who tended to be susceptible to the media and it was through them that the media's effects were transmitted. In the two-step flow model of mass communication ideas and attitudes are said 'to flow *from* radio and print *to* opinion leaders and *from them* to the less active sections of the population' (p. 32). This process is by no means automatic however, and Katz and Lazarsfeld had a far more modest conception of media effects than earlier theorists, one which emphasised personal *decisions* made by opinion leaders as a result of their greater *exposure* to the media than non-leaders. In practice the link between exposure and decisions was quite complex. While opinion leaders usually devoted more time to books and magazines, radio and the cinema, they differed in the extent to which they gave credit to these experiences in making up their own minds. In each of the four main areas in which opinion leaders influenced the attitudes and choices of others – in the buying of food and household goods, in fashion, in going to see a film, and in judgments about current affairs and politics – the results suggested that there was a unique pattern of interpersonal contact with distinct leaders in each sphere. Opinion leaders typically saw their decisions as the outcome of other influences besides the mass media, and only in the area of fashion did they self-consciously rely upon the media in forming their ideas. In short, this research suggested that the impact of the media was far from being as straightforward and direct as previous theories had claimed.

Whereas the hypodermic model saw the media as decisively shaping the ideas and behaviour of an audience made up of individuals who were easily swayed, the two-step flow model revealed the importance of the social relationships amongst audience members in determining their response to the mass media. Katz and Lazarsfeld identified opinion leaders whose views were said by others to be particularly influential. They showed that these key individuals were more exposed to the media than the rest of the population, and that the effects of this exposure were both varied and subtle.

This two-step model has been criticised for dividing media audiences too readily into active and passive members, and also for simplifying the process of influence unnecessarily. As one critic has pointed out 'there is absolutely no reason why there should not be a three-, four-, or five-step flow of communications or more' (Howitt, 1982, p. 21). Against this it should be remembered that opinion leaders only lead on specific issues so that the distinction between leaders and non-leaders is a very fluid one; in fact, this did prompt Katz and Lazarsfeld to suggest that the chains of influence might be even more complex than their evidence was able to show.

A more damaging criticism of this approach is that the authors narrowly equated power with one person's influence over another. A different view of power would stress the importance of political and economic institutions like the State and big business. Radical critics of the two-step flow model have argued that it ignores the fact that the ownership and control of the mass media have become more tightly concentrated than ever before and thus are a potent instrument of class domination (Gitlin, 1978). These questions will be examined in Chapter 3.

The Uses and Gratifications Approach

The two-step flow model did open the way for a better understanding of audiences in the study of media effects, and this was taken up in greater detail by subsequent researchers. In an aside Katz and Lazarsfeld had suggested that it would be worth investigating 'the different kinds of "uses" to which the media are put by leaders . . . as compared with non-leaders' (p. 320). They argued that people actively draw upon the media in order to satisfy various needs and interests – thus, for example, reading popular fiction was particularly marked amongst women who led narrow social lives and this served as 'a substitute for socializing' (p. 378). Later writers tended to abandon Katz and Lazarsfeld's focus on opinion leaders and instead concentrated solely upon the uses made of the media and the satisfaction derived from them by audiences as a whole. Although there are several distinct versions of this theory all of them start from a view of human beings purposefully striving to shape their lives in accord with the needs which they have. A complex psychological make-up is usually assumed, with lower level needs, such as the need for safety and security, and higher level ones like the need for love, acceptance and self-realisation. It is the latter which figure most prominently in people's relation to the mass media. For example, McQuail, Blumler and Brown (1972) have argued that soap operas like *Coronation Street* meet the social need of companionship for some people. 'You feel you know them' was a typical comment from one of the women interviewed about the serial's characters, a remark which suggests the close interweaving of fiction with real life.

Some of the uses made of the media might seem very humdrum but are nevertheless important to the individuals involved: buying and reading a newspaper is a ritual which organises and structures the beginning of one's day, as well as providing up-to-the-minute information and an interpretation of public events. In addition the purchase of a paper like *The Times* might be used to confer social prestige upon the reader. To take another example, Radio Three might be used as musical wallpaper, a background to one's daily tasks, or alternatively as a source of relaxation giving a deep aesthetic experience. The same medium may have different *functions* depending upon the kind of person who is using it and what his or her motives are.

Some critics have argued that uses and gratifications models represent a retreat from the original gains of the two-step flow approach since they are concerned so much with the individual psychology of audience members that they are in danger of losing the social dimension altogether. Not all uses and gratifications models can be dismissed in this way, however. For example, Rosengren and Windahl's (1972) study of media use in two southern Swedish towns tried to test the idea that newspapers, radio and television were turned to by some people as a 'functional alternative' when the possibilities for 'face-to-face interaction with real, living human beings' were either blocked or reduced. This meant extensive investigation into the life-styles and behaviour patterns of audiences. Yet even where this is the case it can be argued that such models are far too speculative to be of much value. They usually take the results of audience interviews as evidence of basic, underlying human needs as if this was all the proof that was necessary. That this is not so is shown by the wide variety in the lists of needs that researchers have produced, there being little agreement about what these basic needs are. Again, users of the mass media are said to be extremely purposeful in their viewing, reading or listening. However, generalisations of this kind ignore the extent to which activities like watching television are often casual and un-planned. And where particular programmes are sought out it may be more a matter of their general popularity and reputation (as reflected in TV audience ratings) than of individuals with certain specific needs trying to gratify them with appropriate programmes.

The uses and gratifications approach was, however, a new departure in the study of the mass media and their audiences. It emphasised the selective way in which people make the media a part of their everyday lives and by so doing are able to satisfy a variety of social needs and desires.

Effects? What Effects?

Both the two-step flow model and the uses and gratifications approaches arose in reaction to the hypodermic syringe theory and, as a result, they share certain common features despite their differences. Where the hypodermic theory overstated the media's impact by con-ceiving of effects too simplistically and was easily discredited by a lack of evidence, its two successors tended to lose sight of the media having any real effect at all. In the two-step flow model the media's influence was placed at one remove from the majority of the audience and even for opinion leaders the connection was a weak one, a matter of 'exposure'. By contrast, the uses and gratifications approaches put the media almost entirely at the audience's beck and call since it was for individuals themselves to determine what role the media were to play in their lives. In both cases effects coming directly from the media were seen to be on the whole negligible.

This was the orthodox view in the sociology of the mass media until the late 1960s. By this time, however, things were slowly starting to change. Quite why this happened would take another book, but certainly, as so often in scientific thinking, the accumulation of weaknesses and discrepancies in existing theories together with the rise of new styles of research combined to lead to a paradigm shift (see Kuhn, 1962). In the rest of this section, I will look at some of these weaknesses.

As Katz and Lazarsfeld themselves pointed out in their book *Personal Influence* 'there are a variety of possible effects that the mass media may have upon society'. Most research, their own included, has been preoccupied with only one: short-term changes in attitudes and opinion. In Stuart Hall's words 'switches of choice – between advertised consumer goods or between presidential candidates – were viewed as a paradigm case of measureable influence and effect' (Hall, 1982, p. 59). This gives the rather misleading impression 'that the media are quite ineffectual' which is only true for one kind of effect. There are other kinds, 'predominantly of a long term sort' which, as Katz and Lazarsfeld admit 'have barely been looked into'. These 'promise to reveal the potency of the mass media' much more than the short-run effects previously studied (p. 19).

Why is it so misleading to concentrate upon changes in attitudes? Partly this is because the concept of 'attitudes' that has been used is a very limited one, as is shown by the way in which they have been investigated. A before-and-after methodology was employed in which people were asked about their changes of mind on a particular issue, and, if so, how they had been influenced. Where their attitudes remained unaltered, the assumption was made that they had not been influenced. Not only does this ignore the possibility 'that a respondent had begun to "change her mind" on a given issue, only to be persuaded back to the original position by personal influences, or, directly, by mass media'. It also fails to consider the relationship between the media and the original set of beliefs, values and opinions which form the baseline against which changes in attitude are measured (Gitlin, 1978, p. 215).

At the very least we can expect the media to play a key role in creating a web of opinions and beliefs around new issues, especially where there are no alternative sources of information. Indeed, Katz and Lazarsfeld themselves reported findings that were quite at odds with their general argument. Thus, 58% of the changes of opinion they studied 'were apparently made without involving any remembered personal contact, and were, very often, dependent upon the mass media' (p. 142). Similar discrepancies have been detected in the earlier study of the 1940 American election. What all this suggests is that the idea of there being some kind of direct media effect was abandoned much too quickly.

Cultural Effects Theory

More recent work has led to a re-thinking of the nature of effects. Cultural effects theory leads us to see the media in a different light and to draw fresh insights from older studies (see Tudor, 1979).

This approach assumes that the media can have important effects on their audiences. However, these effects are not the immediate changes of opinion studied by earlier researchers, but rather the slow, cumulative build-up of beliefs and values through which we understand the world. For example, feminist writers have argued that the kinds of images of women with which the media surround us have had a major influence on our ideas of what women are like and how they should behave. In order to study the influence of the media in terms of cultural effects it is important to analyse the content of the media. We have to see how these images are put together or constructed: to ask, for example, how such types as 'the dumb blonde' in TV films are created out of styles of dress, speech mannerisms, and the like. To understand this fully we would also need to analyse the plot and the portrayal of characters in a story which used this kind of figure. We return to some of these issues in the next chapter.

Cultural effects theory does not look at such images in isolation. The influence of the media will also depend upon the social situation of the audience. For example, the same film shown to working class teenagers and middle class, middle-aged businessmen may well have very different effects on the two audiences. They will interpret the content of the film in terms of their social class subcultures, with reference to their social situations, and in terms of the experiences of their age group. The cultural effects approach seeks to bring together both the way in which meanings are created by the media and the way in which these relate differently to the cultures of particular social groups.

The Return of the Martians

Orson Welles' Martians have already put in an appearance earlier in the book. Now I want to re-introduce you to them in order to show how the idea of a cultural effect can be used to make sense of the way the media work.

On the face of it the story of the 'invasion from Mars' would seem to fit in well with the hypodermic theory: a single immediate and dramatic effect. Certainly at the time when Hadley Cantril's study of these events was published in 1940 this theory was still the dominant perspective, although, significantly, it was on the brink of a severe decline. It is, however, a tribute to the carefulness of Cantril's research that his book *The Invasion from Mars* shows just how complex the real explanation was. Despite the fact that the idea of a cultural effect was not developed until much later several points in his analysis seem to give support to this idea. To justify this claim I shall have to sketch in the background to the broadcast.

First of all, it is important to be clear about the scale of the panic that ensued. The Orson Welles play was part of a regular series, 'The Mercury Theatre on the Air', carried by the Columbia Broadcasting System, America's largest radio network. This meant an audience of six million people spread right across the country from California to New York State. Of these about a million, or one-sixth of those listening, believed it to be a real invasion. What we need to know, therefore, is not just why the broadcast had the effect it did, but why only some listeners were taken in and not others.

The core of Cantril's investigation was based upon detailed interviews with 135 people who had heard the broadcast, of whom over 100 had been upset by it, together with the results of two large national surveys of people who had tuned in to the broadcast. One factor seems to have been especially important in distinguishing those who panicked from those who did not: namely, that the former had a tendency to begin listening to the programme after it had started. A national survey carried out by CBS showed that only 12% of those who had listened from the very beginning were misled. Tuning in late was as common-place then amongst radio audiences as it probably is now for television viewers. The listeners cannot choose which programmes will be made available and when, but must pick from a pre-arranged menu.

On the night of October 30th 1938 the Mercury Theatre was competing with one of the most popular radio variety shows of the week. People would typically switch stations after the act they wanted to hear had finished and the advertising jingles were just starting, so that they caught the Mercury Theatre broadcast well after the introductory announcements were over. Many of those who were alarmed at what they heard then phoned their non-listening friends who also tuned in, which meant that the panic quickly snowballed.

A second main strand in the explanation of the panic lies in the way in which the Mercury Theatre made use of long-standing cultural expectations about news. At the time of the 'invasion from Mars' nearly three times as many people believed in the dependability of radio news compared to that of newspapers, particularly because of the growing importance of the special news bulletin. Welles and his players tried to achieve an impressive and convincing realism in their broadcast: they virtually started from the question, 'How would a radio news bulletin report a real invasion if one occurred?' and constructed their programme around the answer. As Cantril notes 'the broadcast was so realistic for the first few minutes that it was almost credible to even relatively sophisticated and well informed listeners' (pp. 67–8). The technique the broadcasters used was to move gradually from statements that were quite believable to ones that would be very hard to accept taken in isolation. Thus the story started with reports of 'several explosions of incandescent gas, occurring at regular intervals on the planet Mars' and led on to an account of falling meteorites, setting the scene for the sighting of alien beings. Throughout the drama lifelike details were subtly interspersed to indicate that the narrative was situated in real time and space: references to the weather, 'eastern standard time' and well-known geographical locations. As one of those interviewed was at pains to stress '*if they had mentioned any other places but streets right around here*, I would not have been so ready to believe' (p. 73). In fact, those interviewed in the northern New Jersey area, where the towns mentioned in the broadcast were situated, were far more likely to panic than those who lived further away. To add to the realism, the events in the play were constantly being authenticated by what seemed to be expert witnesses: scientists, army officers and high-ranking government officials.

Finally, the nature of the historical moment in which the 'invasion' happened played its part too. America in the late 1930s was an insecure and anxious nation. Still recovering from the shock of the 1929 financial crash, 'probably more important than anything else' in leading to a feeling of demoralisation, Americans were beset by political worries as they watched the rise of Fascism in Europe and mentally prepared themselves for the growing international crisis to erupt into war (p. 203). Between August and October 1938 radio broadcasts were frequently interrupted by news bulletins about the increasing likelihood of war and, as Cantril comments, 'probably never before in the history of broadcasting had so many people in this country been glued to their sets' (p. 159). Not only were people expecting bad news, but some sort of foreign attack could not be ruled out. Even to those who had listened to the play from the very beginning it was far from implausible to believe that the play itself had been interrupted by a news bulletin, as many did. As a result, legislation was passed to prevent the imitation of news broadcasts for dramatic purposes.

Cantril's argument, then, is that these social factors – the manipulation of the conventions of radio news, together with a generalised sense of uncertainty and hopelessness which had been festering for a decade – combined to inhibit what he calls people's normal 'critical ability', producing a startling, albeit temporary, shock. Critical ability simply refers to the capacity for checking one's experience against other sources of information. Some people either checked badly or failed to check what was happening at all – thus they would turn to other frightened listeners for confirmation of what they had heard generating a new and more intensely collective form of fear in the process. Cantril rejects any claim that the panic can be explained by the innate stupidity or neuroticism of the audience precisely because critical ability is not something which is innate but 'is the result of a particular environment' which has formed the individual. Thus one listener who was not taken in found that the information about the army did not square with his own army experience, even though 'it all sounded perfectly real' (pp. 90–1).

Cantril's research suggests that the 'invasion from Mars' panic can be seen as an example of a cultural effect by the media. It was the life-like quality of the broadcast combined with the social and cultural situation of the listeners which brought about the scare. A panic 'occurs when some highly cherished, rather commonly accepted value is threatened and when no certain elimination of the threat is in sight'. Here the value placed on security and human life was threatened and the 'news' about the 'invasion' offered no hope of the threat being lifted. Cantril argues that the fear triggered off by the panic was 'latent in the general population, not specific to the persons who happened to participate in it'. It was intensified by 'the discrepancy between the whole superstructure of economic, social and political practices and beliefs, and the basic and derived needs of individuals' typical of the troubled 1930s (pp. 199–204). In other words, people's needs were not being met in US society of the 1930s. The tension and anxiety that resulted fuelled the panic. Thus to understand the effect of the media, the relationship between its content, its audience and the social context must be examined.

Mods and Rockers: A Moral Panic

The second example illustrating the idea of a cultural effect is a more recent one – although not recent enough to be considered truly contemporary. Stan Cohen's book *Folk Devils and Moral Panics* was already a bit of an historical curiosity when it appeared in 1972, for the youth groups of the mid-sixties which he described had long since disappeared. Nevertheless his work has become a classic study of the way in which the media contributes to the creation of deviant behaviour.

Cohen's study was inspired by those interactionist theories which draw attention to societal reaction or labelling in their explanations of deviance. Here the stress is upon the way in which deviant acts are identified and publicised by society at large, or powerful groups within it, and thus with 'the *nature, emergence, application* and *consequences* of deviancy labels' (Plummer, 1979, p. 88). Cohen is therefore less concerned with looking for the causes or motives lying behind deviant behaviour as such. Instead he is interested in trying to see how these acts are picked out for special censure and the influence which this has upon the likelihood of further acts occurring. The use and application of deviancy labels not only allows the majority of people to make sense of social life by charting the boundary between right and wrong, it also may produce the very behaviour it is used to condemn – not least by contributing to and confirming the deviant's feeling of self-identity once an initial act has been labelled.

The mass media have an important role in developing the labels by which social problems are publicly recognised. Typically such problems are conveyed to us as a conflict between 'goodies' and 'baddies', or heroes and villains. The hue and cry against such moral outcasts, which is likely to be intensified when society is undergoing a crisis, resembles the old practice of witch-hunting with its scapegoating and persecution. The result is that the social problems represented by modern 'folk devils' become magnified out of all proportion.

The beginning of the Mods and Rockers phenomenon occurred in Clacton, a seaside resort which had traditionally attracted young people from the tougher parts of London, despite the fact that the range of amenities it offered was small. Bad weather meant bad business for local shopkeepers and boredom for the young people, intensifying an atmosphere of mutual suspicion. One wet weekend in Easter 1964 trouble started when 'a few groups started scuffling on the pavements and throwing stones at each other'. Over the weekend there were broken windows, wrecked beach huts and a great deal of noisy riding around on bikes and scooters (p. 29). Though the nature of the disturbance was fairly minor the local police were taken by surprise by the sheer numbers of young people on the streets.

Cohen argues that the vocabulary used by the media wildly inflated any threat these events presented. Even the Assistant Editor of the *Daily Mirror* later acknowledged that these incidents had been 'a little over-reported'. The *Daily Telegraph's* headline proclaimed: 'Day of Terror by Scooter Groups', and the *Daily Express*: 'Youngsters Beat Up Town – 97 Leather Jacket Arrests'. Cohen attempted to gauge the accuracy of the reporting by the national press by comparing it with that of the local papers which gave more detail and avoided making statements that their readers would obviously recognise as false or misleading.

There are three main types of over-reporting: exaggeration or distortion, prediction, and symbolization. *Exaggeration* takes the form of over-estimating such features as the numbers of people involved or the scale of the damage. Emotive language such as 'riot', 'orgy of destruction', 'siege' or 'beat up the town' is used and crucial facts are misrepresented. For example, Cohen's study shows that much emphasis was given to motor-bikes and scooters, yet these were in a minority and 'the majority of young people present came down by train or coach or hitched' (p. 35). Similarly, the reports of violence and vandalism were overwritten. At Clacton just twenty-four of the ninety-seven arrested were charged, and only a couple of these were charged with offences involving violence.

These inflated accounts of specific events are also projected into the future in the form of a *prediction* that there will be a repeat performance. For example, witnesses may be asked leading questions about what will happen next time, thus helping to stimulate a self-fulfilling prophecy. Through *symbolization* a whole wealth of associations are built up around certain words and the styles and individuals to which they refer. The Mods' fur-collared anoraks and scooters became visual signs of delinquency and 'became sufficient in themselves to stimulate hostile and punitive reactions' from police and public. Because of the publicity value of labels like 'mod' or 'punk' they are often dubiously applied by the press as a technique for arousing readers' interest. For example, a 1964 headline 'Terror Comes to English Resorts. Mutilated Mod Dead in Park' actually referred to the stabbing of a man in his mid-thirties in a park in the 'resort' of Birmingham!

Cohen argues that the take-off from fairly trivial, if unpleasant, happenings to a full-scale societal alarm constitutes what he calls a 'moral panic'. This has two sides to it. The sparks of the initial deviant behaviour are fanned into something far more serious by lurid reporting which in turn generates an increase in deviance. At the same time representatives of what Cohen terms 'the control culture' – the police, the courts, and members of the local community – start to step up their response. They become less tolerant of flamboyant styles of dress and behaviour amongst young people and are sensitised to be constantly on the look-out for hooliganism. In the atmosphere of hysteria which is created innocent individuals may easily be harassed or even arrested, and the increased activity on the part of the control culture is itself taken as showing the seriousness of the problem. The control culture at such moments is likely to be extended beyond routine law enforcement as new institutions like local action committees come into being and questions about the state of the nation are asked in parliament. The spread of deviance due to the attention it receives and the escalation in the reaction to it from the control culture feed on each other to produce an 'amplification spiral' in which each new occurrence adds to the problem and confirms each of the participants in what they are doing. While a moral panic is by no means inevitable in such circumstances, once started it is difficult to stop. In this case a cycle of holiday disturbances was set in motion across England which continued until 1967 by which time Mods and Rockers as social phenomena were practically dead.

Cohen used letters to the press and the minutes of council and parliamentary debates to document the societal reaction. He also interviewed members of the public, including a survey of attitudes amongst those who were formally concerned with the problem of delinquency: headmasters, lawyers, magistrates and youth workers. As Cohen himself admits, this was the least satisfactory part of his research in that it was not a comprehensive study of public opinion, but his results do make some interesting points. The analysis of the letters suggested that the Mods and Rockers were a symbol for 'a whole pattern in which pregnant schoolgirls, CND marches, beatniks, long hair, contraceptives in slot machines, purple hearts and smashing up telephone kiosks were all inextricably intertwined' (pp. 54–5). The interviews reflected this generally negative view of Mods and Rockers, but were far less alarmist. Indeed, many people were 'explicitly critical of the role of the media' (p. 69). Cohen's samples were very small and the questions he asked were fairly limited, but they do suggest that the reactions in society at large are not all of a piece – people had reservations about the media's portrayal of young people based on their own beliefs and experiences, despite their general acceptance of media imagery.

Cohen draws the following conclusions from his research. 'Folk devils', in this case Mods and Rockers, are central to the creation of a 'moral panic'. A 'moral panic' occurs when people fear that the major values and institutions of society are under attack, as many did in Britain in the mid-1960s. Young people fit the bill as 'folk devils', 'visible reminders of what we (youth especially) should not be'. They are easy to identify, relatively powerless and it is fairly simple to exaggerate certain aspects of their behaviour so as to make them appear as a threat to society. They become scapegoats, an easy target for the fear and hate of many people in the wider society. The media play an important role in whipping up moral panics, identifying folk devils, amplifying their deviance, and providing targets for popular anxieties. Again the effects of the media are explained in terms of their audience and the social context.

So far we have looked at two examples of cultural effects: Cantril's study of 'the invasion from Mars' and Cohen's work on moral panics in the mid-sixties. Both suggest that cultural effects are far from uniform: in complex industrial societies media effects will partly be shaped by the social situation and experience of audience members. For example, our sense of identity as a man or woman, one's feeling of class membership or one's loyalty to one's town or region are all likely to colour our response to what we find in the media. Yet neither of the studies examines this source of variation in cultural effects in any detail. This suggests that a more sophisticated version of the cultural effects model is required, one which takes account of the social variety of the audience. This can be seen from the work of David Morley.

Researching Audience Response

David Morley's research is one of the best recent attempts to study the variation in audience response to the media. In a project on the reception of the TV current affairs programme 'Nationwide' he has considerably refined our knowledge of the cultural meaning of television. This returns us to a point made earlier in relation to Cantril's work on 'the invasion from Mars': that the power which a symbol or message possesses will derive from the social and cultural context in which it is seen or heard, in that case from the anxieties of a demoralised pre-war America.

In his book *The 'Nationwide' Audience* (1980) Morley shows how careful and sensitive interviewing can reveal differences in audience response that are neither random nor purely personal but systematically tied in with one's place in the social structure. Morley carried out group discussions with 29 different sets of people after letting them watch a video recording of *Nationwide* programmes. The groups were deliberately chosen to represent a wide range of social and educational backgrounds and usually consisted of between five and ten people. The decision to go for group interviews followed from the conviction that it was misleading to talk to individuals outside of any social context. The groups were made up of people who were peers in some respect and, because they were based on classes in schools, colleges or universities, the groups had been in existence for some time. They included bank managers, full-time trade union officials, apprentice printers, engineers and metallurgists and general literacy students. Morley sought to conduct the interviews in as non-directive a way as possible, allowing his respondents to define the situation for themselves and to express their views naturally. Only in the later stages did he move towards more specific and more probing questions.

A few of the group discussions can be singled out to illustrate his findings. For example, what is striking about the groups of bank managers interviewed is their complete acceptance of the content of the programme. Their criticisms were chiefly directed at the programme's style or what has come to be called its 'mode of address' – that is the way it puts its message across to us. *Nationwide's* mode of address was determinedly populist and down-to-earth in its approach, representing ordinary people against experts, officials and 'red tape'. It was precisely this to which the bank managers objected, finding it 'embarrassing' and 'patronising' and 'talking down . . . even to the lowest paid worker' (pp. 106–7). By contrast, a group of shop stewards were approving of this populist style. However, they were so incensed by the implicit assumptions behind what was being said in the programme that they produced a critical running commentary while they were viewing it. For them, *Nationwide's* treatment of the 1977 Budget made it sound 'as if everyone's aspiring to be middle management' (pp. 112–118). As a final example, a group of young black students at a college of further education found the programme irrelevant to their world. As Morley points out 'their particular experience of family structures among a black, working class, inner city community is simply not accounted for' (pp. 122). Thus, when they criticise the programme for not dealing with the average family, in terms of their experience of families this was true. Their criticisms struck out at one of *Nationwide's* proudest claims: that it represented the national community of individual citizens. The liveliness and immediacy cultivated by the language of 'Nationwide' passed these young black people by and consequently they found the programme was soporific and dull. They did not feel themselves a part of the 'people' *Nationwide* was supposedly representing. Instead they saw it as portraying a nation of 'middle class shoppers and businessmen' (p. 118).

Morley argues that the kinds of audience responses he discovered can be broadly categorised into three main types, according to how the broadcast is 'read' or understood: (i) viewers can endorse the dominant common-sense values built into the programme which tacitly justify the status quo, (ii) they can generally accept the meaning of the programme as given but seek to modify or adjust it by making exceptions or qualifications in line with their own social situation, or (iii) they can oppose it. Morley refers to these respectively as dominant, negotiated and oppositional readings or decodings of the programme. There are also variations *within* each of these types of readings. Clearly the bank managers and the shop stewards represent the extremes of acceptance and opposition, yet the black students too produced their own oppositional reading of the programme different from that made by the shop stewards. While the black students and the shop stewards can be said to share a common class position, argues Morley, the precise character of their response derives from variations in ideas and experiences, in one case from trade union radicalism and in the other from black youth culture.

Morley's work makes a number of important points. Audiences are not passive receivers of media messages. They actively interpret what they see and hear. To understand their interpretations we must analyse both the content of the media and the social backgrounds and experience of audience members. Media effects are the result of a complex interaction between these factors.

Violence and the Media

Now that I have given an outline of what is involved in talking about cultural effects and looked at some of its implications for research I want to return to an issue mentioned earlier, that of the impact of violence in the media. As I said then, this is a perennial debate. Because of the indignation it excites amongst people and because of the questions it raises about the social responsibility of the media it hits the headlines again and again, with each new research study being treated as a human interest story in its own right. Part of the problem is that there is so much research and most of it is inconclusive and contradictory. In the remainder of this chapter I want to look at some of the difficulties with this research and to see if we can use the notion of a cultural effect to help us assess its strengths and weaknesses.

Problems of Method

It is easy to get lost in the maze of research and some commentators have yielded to the temptation of supposing that it is a hopeless venture to even try to prove that such effects exist. TV campaigner Mary Whitehouse, speaking in 1970, recommended that we should trust to the certainty of commonsense instead, for it tells us 'that the screening of violence, horror, shock and obscenity into the home . . . can have nothing but a destructive effect upon our sensitivities and our society' (quoted in Tracey and Morrison, 1979, p. 85). One of the reasons why this view is so appealing is precisely because research into media effects is very difficult to carry out.

Three different sources of data have been used to investigate the effects of the portrayal of violence on the screen. These are clinical case studies, laboratory experiments and field studies. None of them is foolproof and to some extent their employment depends upon the perspective from which one is working.

As Eysenck and Nias have pointed out, the clinical case study 'is popularly regarded as the most convincing and impressive, but is scientifically of least interest' (Eysenck and Nias, 1980, p. 65). This approach looks at the biographies of individuals who have been convicted of anti-social acts which seem to have been influenced by particular films or programmes. Now such a line of investigation seems to have a great deal of plausibility. When a 17-year old boy tries to murder his father with a meat cleaver after watching a film on TV in which a boy kills his father, it is hard not to be both shocked and convinced, especially when the boy confesses to the police: 'It's just that when I watch television I sometimes imagine myself committing murders and thinking I can get away with it' (quoted in Eysenck and Nias, p. 67). But a moment's reflection will make us want to ask for more proof. Might this not be a case of a seriously disturbed individual who is likely to act violently anyway, and for whom television is little more than an excuse? After all, the very fact that this is an exceptional case and that the overwhelming majority of young viewers are not influenced in this way might make us wonder whether other factors are not at work here. The case study method can assemble much interesting information but is never likely to be conclusive simply because it does not allow us to compare similar individuals and to tease out why some people seem to be susceptible while most are not.

This strongly suggests that in order to study the effect of violence in the media we need to devise controlled experiments in which conditions can be carefully managed by the investigator so as to isolate the factors in which she or he is interested and assess whether any of them is causing a change in behaviour. In other words, we try to find out what will happen in a highly specific set of circumstances and generalise from our findings to other situations. Laboratory experiments in social science have largely been the province of psychologists, and fall outside the scope of this book. From a sociological standpoint their precision of method is achieved at the cost of excluding the relevant details of real social settings so that behaviour in the laboratory is highly artificial. *The Williams Report on Obscenity and Film Censorship* which appeared in 1979 found the evidence provided by experimental studies subject to severe drawbacks. It noted that 'since criminal and antisocial behaviour cannot itself, for both practical and ethical reasons, be experimentally produced or controlled, the observations must be made on some surrogate or related behaviour, often expressed on a representational object, in some fictional or "pretend" context' (Williams, 1981, p. 65). For example, in experimental studies of the imitation of violence by children after watching films or TV, special toys or dolls are given to the children and their behaviour towards them is used as a measure of the programme's effect. A comparison is made between the level of aggressiveness towards the dolls of those children who had been exposed to the programme and those who had not. The difficulty here is that the dolls have been deliberately designed to invite rough play and are therefore hardly a true guide to interpersonal violence. Indeed, those children who have prior experience of the dolls seem to engage in less imitative aggression than others. A further problem is that only the effect of short doses of film or TV violence can be investigated in this way if people are not to become permanent experimental subjects. Thus as Eysenck and Nias admit 'it is not . . . possible to study the effect of years of exposure to television under laboratory conditions' (Eysenck and Nias, 1980, p. 75). Long-term effects could only be studied as a series of brief exposures to violent material, a solution which they accept is a compromise.

Field studies comprise a variety of methods, including the use of observation, interviews and questionnaires, but all aim at getting close to social behaviour as it naturally happens. Compared to the experiment they are very inexact since it is hard to select people for study in such a way as to be sure that the results obtained were due to one particular cause rather than a large number of other possible factors. In order to meet criticisms of this kind some of the more positivist researchers have tried to approximate to experimental rigour as closely as possible when designing their studies. An example of a field study which does this is discussed in the following section.

William Belson: TV and Teenage Violence

In his book *Television Violence and the Adolescent Boy* (1978) William Belson carried out in-depth interviews with 1,565 boys in London aged between 12 and 17 years. The purpose of this large-scale field study, which was funded by the US Columbia Broadcasting System, was to test the hypothesis that the boys' exposure to television violence was a cause of their involvement in acts of violence. The research design he used was extremely sophisticated and complex. Firstly, he attempted to eliminate alternative explanations by matching the boys in his sample on a wide variety of factors which might conceivably have caused an increase in violent behaviour, and then systematically comparing groups that were alike except for one single characteristic, much as one would do in a controlled experiment. Secondly, he gathered his data in three stages in order that the answers to his questions could be checked and cross-checked by obtaining information in different ways and under different conditions. For example, the boys were interviewed both at home with their parents and individually at a research centre. By comparing boys who had had above-average exposure to television violence with those who had only a low exposure, Belson claimed strong support for his hypothesis. Thus because 'high exposure to television violence increases the degree to which boys engage in serious violence' he felt confident in recommending that 'steps should be taken as soon as possible to achieve a substantial reduction in the total amount of violence being presented on television' (Belson, 1978, pp. 15–20).

For all the undoubtedly painstaking effort that went into this research (Belson even sees fit to mention that the interviews 'spanned both hot and cold weather'), it has attracted its fair share of criticism. Some social scientists have been frankly incredulous of Belson's finding that boys who were heavily exposed to television violence committed 49% more acts of serious violence than those who had little exposure. So strong are the claims that Belson makes that it is worth looking in more detail at the problems that his work faces.

In the first place, there are inconsistencies in his results which are never really explained. For example, not only does he show that very violent acts are correlated with watching a lot of television violence, his findings also reveal a correlation between these acts and *all* television viewing. Unfortunately we never really learn why this is so. Similarly, the link between violent behaviour and TV violence is far from being as straightforward as Belson sometimes suggests. Thus, whilst the amount of violent behaviour rises the more violent TV is watched, this relationship reaches a peak and then declines. In other words, as Dennis Howitt has pointed out, it is those who watch a moderate amount of violent TV who are actually the most violent in their behaviour, and 'heavy and light viewers of TV violence alike are less aggressive than middle range viewers'. As Howitt also notes, this means that 'it is equally logical to argue that we can reduce aggression in society by *increasing* the amount of violence watched as by decreasing it' (Howitt, 1982, pp. 98–9).

A further set of problems concern the measurements that Belson took in order to assess the violent behaviour of the boys and the level of violence in TV programmes. Murdock and McCron have argued that both are suspect, particularly because they rely very heavily on memory. To find out how exposed the boys were to televised violence Belson presented them with a list of over one hundred programmes shown between one and twelve years earlier and asked them how many times they remembered seeing them. This has the drawback of producing data that are based in several cases on recollections of viewing experiences which took place when the boys were only a few years old, even allowing for the imperfections of ordinary memory. Moreover, Belson attempted to devise an independent and objective measure of the level of violence in the TV programmes by getting panels of adults to judge them, and then turning these judgments into a ten point scale. Yet as Murdock and McCron point out, 'we know from other audience studies that there is a considerable divergence between the preferences of middle-class adults and those of teenage boys, especially those from working-class backgrounds' (Murdock & McCron, 1979, p. 57). This may explain some of the oddities in the results. For example, Westerns were found to be causally related to aggressiveness, while science fiction programmes were not, despite the fact that the judges rated a programme like *Dr. Who* as more violent than Westerns like *Rawhide* or *High Chaparral*.

The measure of violent behaviour by the boys is open to similar criticisms. It relied upon self-report data thus raising once again problems of bad memory or exaggeration. To help the boys remember,

Belson introduced details about the circumstances surrounding typical violent acts of different kinds. Unfortunately, once this data was obtained, it was categorised in a very abstract way which ignored all reference to the context which made the act of violence intelligible in the first place. Thus the category of 'serious violence' includes statements like 'I busted the telephone in a telephone box' and quite different ones like 'I deliberately hit a boy in the face with a broken bottle' and 'I fired a revolver at someone'. Questions of context and motivation are avoided and 'difference in *type* between these acts are submerged in favour of totting up the number of acts reported and grading them for seriousness' (Murdock & McCron, 1979, p. 58).

An Alternative View of TV Violence

In spite of Belson's claim that his enquiry 'would be based upon *normal* long term exposure to television violence, upon behaviour as it *normally* occurs and upon attitudes as they *normally* develop', there are serious doubts as to whether this was so (Belson, 1978, p. 10). Critics have argued that his research is insensitive to the realities of contemporary youth cultures. Indeed his method of selecting individual boys from the whole of London fails to take sub-cultural groups into account at all, and therefore makes little use of an important body of theory and research in this field. By contrast, ethnographic studies using in-depth interviews try to show how patterns of leisure amongst young people are rooted in the class cultures of local neighbourhoods. Dave Robins and Phil Cohen's work on young East Londoners, for example, begins to answer questions which only puzzle Belson. At one point Belson notes that 'parents had been full of stories about the imitation by their sons of Kung Fu type violence' but his own impression is that imitation occurs only 'under certain circumstances' which he never really specifies (Belson, pp. 524–6). Robins and Cohen in their book *Knuckle Sandwich* (1978) document the interest in martial arts amongst both boys *and* girls (the latter ignored by Belson). They show that this is no simple matter of imitation, however, particularly since this interest was shared by those who were members of fighting gangs and those who were not. Robins and Cohen argue that it is the kids' sense of being descendants of earlier youth groups like the teddy boys as well as their half-admiring relationship to the adult criminal subcultures in their locality which creates an interest in the martial arts and gives special meaning to media output. This returns us to David Morley's point that programmes are interpreted in line with social experience and social background. The effects are mediated through the culture of audience members. They are therefore 'cultural effects'. Since the culture of audience members varies, it is thus hard to support the kind of blanket assessments of media violence which are frequently given.

This chapter has reviewed the main approaches to media effects, and has suggested that it is necessary to study both the kinds of pictures of the world which are painted by the mass media, and the varied ways in which this imagery is interpreted by different social groups. In other words, it has been argued that media effects are cultural effects which shape our understanding of the social world in line with our background and experience. So far, however, only very brief examples of the actual content of the media have been given. The next chapter will deal more fully with the sociological analysis of media content.

Chapter Two

Media Imagery and Representations

The media now provide us with a continuous flow of images and information. We take this for granted, but in the early days of the mass media things were very different. When the first American newspaper appeared in Boston in 1690 its editor proclaimed his intention to publish news regularly – once a month. (Boorstin, 1962). In modern industrial societies we expect news to be up-to-the-minute and to have drama at the turn of a switch. The media are massively present in our lives and it is this that gives them their cultural effect: they feed into our world-views and our culture, and help to shape them. This chapter looks at the kinds of view of the social world offered by the media, and the questions these raise.

Representations, Stereotypes and Ideology

All human culture is based upon the use of signs and symbols, since it is these that allow us to communicate and make sense of our environment. For example, the people of north eastern Thailand classify insects into those which can be eaten and those which cannot. We rely upon such categories and imagery in order to produce, record and store information. Sociologists sometimes refer to these as *representations*. The classic French sociologist Emile Durkheim used this term to include 'drawings, symbols of all sorts, formulae, whether written or spoken', our conception of animate and inanimate objects, and even the actual objects themselves, as for instance when a goat symbolically serves as a regimental mascot. He argued that 'essentially social life is made up of representations' and that they constrain our thought and behaviour (Durkheim, 1952, p. 40). The media are an important source of these collective representations for they constantly map out for us the contours of our culture and society.

Durkheim tended to write as if collective representations were shared by everyone in much the same way. He stressed social integration rather than social conflict and failed to emphasise that our representations may become a matter for dispute. For example, the 'harmless fun' of page three of the *Sun* can be seen as a symbol of degradation from a feminist perspective, precisely because it conveys a view of women as mere playthings of men that is socially limited and confining. Feminist writers would argue for more positive representations of women in which they have effective control over their own bodies and are not simply used to sell newspapers to men. Representations are a necessary part of social life, but this does not prevent us from being able to choose between different kinds of representations and trying to change them.

The term *stereotype* is often used to indicate those representations which are misleading or offensive. A stereotype is a conventional way of representing someone or something so that our view of them becomes 'frozen' or fixed and may give rise to social prejudices. Stereotypes mark out the acceptable boundaries of our social world: they typically point to those who do not fully belong. Thus women, blacks and homosexuals frequently figure as stereotypes and this reflects their inferior position in society. For example, stereotypes of black characters in films as 'Uncle Toms', faithful servants, comedians or minstrels, and wild savages conjure up a whole history of slavery, discrimination and colonialism. Stereotypes like these are a potent vehicle for *ideology*; in other words, they are a source and support for ideas which legitimate powerful vested interests in society, such as the social advantages enjoyed by whites at the expense of blacks. Ideologies are sets of ideas which justify social disadvantages and injustices, whether these ideas are deliberately put forward by privileged sections of society or not. As we shall see later, a number of writers argue that ideology arises out of the structure of society itself, rather than from the self-interested designs of some of its members.

This chapter continues by looking in more detail at media representations dealing with (i) sex and gender, and (ii) race.

Representations of Sex and Gender

Studies of the ways in which women are represented in the mass media have, until recently, been few and far between. With the recent revival in feminist ideas, however, this area of research has assumed increasing importance. Its neglect is all the more surprising when one remembers that women are identified by media professionals as a specialised market for journalism and fiction. A magazine like *Woman's Own*, for example, was being read by nearly a quarter of all women in the UK in 1981, and even 13% of British men regularly look at a woman's weekly.

These publications are deeply contradictory. On the one hand they speak to women's interests – for example, by providing a forum for information and advice; while on the other, they seem to reinforce narrow and unrewarding feminine roles. Advertisements often present glamorous female images, yet their visual conventions subtly imply the disadvantaged position of women in society. Erving Goffman's study of gender representations in advertisements found that 'men tend to be located higher than women' and 'women are pictured on floors and beds more than men'. He points out that 'lowering oneself physically in some form or other of prostration' is a way of representing inferiority and subservience: it is 'a classic stereotype of deference' (Goffman, 1979, pp. 40–2).

It can be argued that women's magazines traditionally fulfil an important pastoral role by offering women solutions to the problems they experience in their everyday lives. Bridget Fowler (1979) has suggested that women's magazine stories took over one of the key tasks of religion, namely to state a moral code laying down 'how life can and should be lived'. She examined a sample of domestic melodramas taken from popular twopenny magazines like *People's Friend* and *Home Chat* between mid-1929 and the late 1930s, which were read mainly by working class women. Her aim was to see how these moral ideas were put across.

Fowler found domestic melodramas to be a predominantly optimistic genre: they centre upon the pursuit of romantic love and a number of obstacles have to be surmounted before there can be a happy ending. These obstacles often reveal the ideological assumptions behind the stories. An example of this is the treatment of bigamy in some of these tales. In a typical plot the heroine is an unhappily married woman who meets her true love and whose marriage is therefore an obstacle to her real romantic happiness. She cannot get divorced since this was unacceptable in the 20s and 30s. Later in the story she discovers that her husband has committed bigamy. The marriage is not legal and binding and she is now free to marry her true love with whom she lives happily ever after. The ideological message presented in this kind of story supports the conventional morality of the time: love finds its rightful place in a proper marriage. Indeed Fowler notes that 'in the stories bigamy is viewed as so shameful that horrific sacrifices on the part of the good are required before the social order can once again be restored' – thus bigamously-conceived children always die. The institution of marriage and a woman's place within it are reaffirmed against the unthinkable alternatives of divorce and separation.

The barriers of social class are another obstacle to romantic happiness. Yet as Fowler points out, within the class structure described in these stories there is frequent social mobility and the wealth of the rich is depicted 'more as a *decorative trimming* than a vital social difference'. As a result heroines may happily marry into a higher social class free from snobbery and social discrimination. In other words, class and gender are imagined in such a way as to legitimate each other and inequalities of wealth and position are never challenged. Because they appeared at a time when Britain was experiencing a severe economic depression, Fowler argues that the ideological view of the world contained in these stories served as a 'bulwark against despair and resentment', a kind of consolation.

Some studies of more recent examples of this kind of fiction have suggested that it puts forward simple stereotypes of women which its readers try to live up to. For instance, Adams and Laurikietis claim that representations of women in romance stories fall into two groups: 'the "good", sexually innocent woman, who gets her reward – her man' and 'the "bad" woman, who is often sexually experienced, and makes demands' (Adams and Laurikietis, 1976, p. 48). Janet Woollacott (1980) has taken issue with this argument, because it underestimates the skill and variety of much of this writing and assumes that women readers are gullible and unsophisticated. Taking the example of Georgette Heyer's Regency romance, *The Grand Sophy,* Woollacott demonstrates that this novel is a pleasurable read for women because it uses an unconventional heroine who outrages everyone around her to make fun of the stereotypes and clichés associated with this kind of story. However, this makes the ideological message of the text very subtle: to recognise this we have to become consciously aware that the admirable independence of the heroine and the equality which she enjoys with the hero is only made possible by Sophy's having her own fortune. In other words, the author makes us forget the usual patriarchal property relationships of the period: she makes her readers identify with the heroine and think of men and women as already socially equal when clearly they are not – then or now. The heroine may be a positive and therefore an enjoyable representation of a woman but it is one that is based on fantasy. Yet it is far from being a crude stereo-type. Plot and characterisation can convey ideology in fiction in complex and attractive ways. Fowler and Woollacott tend to suggest that authors too are unconscious victims of the very ideology which their stories encourage, since these ideas are so widespread in modern societies.

Marjorie Ferguson's book *Forever Feminine* (1983) is the fullest account of women's magazines to date. She argues that they celebrate the fact of being a woman and also promote the ideal of the exemplary or outstanding woman. This is a sacred ideal rather like a religion with its own beliefs and rituals 'attached to beautification, child-rearing, housework and cooking'. Ferguson calls this 'the cult of femininity'. Like Durkheim she is interested in showing how collective representations hold a social group together. Yet she also recognises that women's magazines are both a social and an economic phenomenon: for the enhanced sense of female solidarity they promote is part of a profit-making exercise.

Ferguson identifies the shared values which underpin the cult of femininity by analysing the content of the three best-selling women's magazines in Britain between 1949 and 1974: *Woman, Woman's Own* and *Woman's Weekly*. She looked at a number of different types of items – fiction, problem pages, features and beauty columns – and found that they were constructed around eleven main themes. These included the importance of emotional expression in women's lives as against rationality and logical thought, feminine unpredictability and mysteriousness, and the value of youth. However, two themes turned out to be dominant time and again: firstly, the theme of love and marriage, 'getting and keeping your man', and secondly, the theme of self-improvement or self-perfection, the virtue of individual achievement. Ferguson carried out a follow-up study for the period 1979–80 to see whether this same order of dominant themes had continued. In fact, they were reversed: in the 1979–80 magazines the theme of self-improvement moved from second to first place as the chief message associated with the cult. Ferguson argues that there is a tension between these two themes since the duties of a wife and mother are not easily reconciled with 'showing you are someone in your own right'. The magazines play down this conflict. Indeed, the theme of the working wife being a bad wife, which was prevalent in the 1950s, had been overturned by the 1970s, when a reader would be reminded that she was 'Not Just a Housewife' (pp. 54–5).

Although the late 1950s were a golden age for British women's weeklies, between 1958 and 1981 their combined weekly sales fell from 12 million to 6.1 million copies. This change is accelerating in the 1980s when women's magazines face increased competition not only from elsewhere in Fleet Street but from the expanding electronic media too. Ferguson also notes that the success of the theme of female self-perfection may carry with it its own built-in obsolescence: the more women are able to control their own lives, the less they need to rely upon the advice offered by women's magazines. Changes in values, together with social and technical changes such as the rationalisation of domestic work through the increasing use of freezers and shopping at large-scale supermarkets may, Ferguson argues, render much of that advice superfluous. Yet the magazines which have survived are those which have maintained the traditional trappings of the cult. Their message is still that 'women are uniquely different' and 'require separate treatment and instruction in ways that men do not' (p. 190). While their audience is smaller than it once was, it is no less committed.

This section has briefly outlined some of the research into the representations of women in the media, particularly those found in women's magazines. It suggests that women's views of themselves and their place in society are to a degree moulded and reinforced by such representations. This process is ideological in the sense that it supports powerful vested interests in society – those of men – and so helps to maintain the subordination of women. Ferguson, however, sees a positive side to the 'cult of femininity' presented by women's magazines. In her view it provides collective representations which contribute to a sense of self-esteem and belonging amongst women, a source of support that is often lacking in the wider society. She even goes so far as to compare these magazines with the women's movement: both are 'directed towards raising the consciousness of women', but while women's magazines aim to make their readers more aware about 'getting, if not keeping, a man', the women's movement is concerned with 'getting the better, or at least the equal, of him' (p. 187).

Race and the Media

In race relations, the media provides information where public knowledge is fragmentary. Although there are some two million black people in Britain, they live mainly in a few major population centres and therefore the white majority's contact with them is often slight. Research into the media's treatment of race over the years has suggested that its reporting has been limited in its themes and negative in its content. Hartmann *et al* (1974) in their analysis of the national press between 1963 and 1970 found that race relations coverage tended to focus upon signs of racial conflict and to give very little attention to the access of black people to housing, education and employment, 'competition for which would seem to be among the underlying roots of tension' (p. 132). Race was usually associated with trouble, as in the cliché 'race riot'. Certainly it is possible to show that the use of this kind of stereotyped language by the press has sometimes resulted in gross misrepresentations. For example, the *Evening News'* front page headline 'SCHOOL MOBS IN LONDON RACE RIOT' in July 1973 was later censured by the Press Council as 'inaccurate' and 'unjustified' following an official complaint; 'the riot' was, in fact, a fight between two rival schools and not two different ethnic groups (Braham, 1982, p. 273). Stories like this give a highly ideological and misleading view of black people as a problem and a menace, and helps to perpetuate their social disadvantages.

Troyna's more comprehensive study of the local and national press and local radio revealed that between 1976 and 1978 reporting about black people was chiefly organised around the idea of 'the outsider within' (Troyna, 1981, p. 45). Nevertheless, despite a big decline in New Commonwealth immigration into Britain, 'immigration' was the second major topic in the press reporting of race, accounting for 11.7% of all material devoted to this item. What was also striking was the convergence upon the same issues and themes by the different media. The impression created was still basically negative and ideological: in 'the media's representation of reality, cultural differences are disparaged and the black population seen as a problem to, and essentially different from the mainstream of the society' (p. 80). Editorials may emphasise the need for harmony and tolerance, but they are outweighed by the quite different treatment given to news stories. Troyna carried out a survey of public attitudes in order to see whether reporting had influenced popular opinion. His results supported the earlier work of Hartmann *et al*, since the interviews showed that the media had encouraged an ideological belief that black people were a source of trouble. However, this process of influence was a complex combination of personal experience (including gossip and myth) and media exposure.

Some of the assumptions underlying this type of research have recently been challenged by Peter Braham. Firstly, he argues that it is difficult to tell whether the media promote racial prejudice or merely reflect already existing racist attitudes on the basis of the data which have been presented. For example, he suggests that the impact of Enoch Powell's speeches on the general public is not necessarily to be explained as a result of the negative values typical of media coverage of race. Powell's popular acclaim stemmed from a failure by the media to recognise the extent of the public's fears; in other words, 'anxiety and discontent about race and immigration...had been accorded insufficient attention in the mass media' (Braham, 1982, p. 282). Secondly, Braham argues that criticism of the media for neglecting the 'underlying roots' of racial tension misses the point. It assumes that 'if you take away shortages of housing and jobs, race relations will become universally smooth' and under-estimates how deep-rooted an historical phenomenon racism may be (p. 283). Furthermore, to expect the press, radio or TV to always be concerned with lengthy in-depth reporting of the social conditions relevant to issues like race is to mistake the role of the media, since much news is concerned with capturing the short-term and the dramatic for tight editorial deadlines and easy and ephemeral consumption.

However, one reason why the reporting of race by the media can be criticised as misleading and distorted is because both newspapers and TV do claim to present information objectively. The press distinguishes between editorial statements of opinion and factual reporting and maintains that these should always be kept separate. As the old newspaper adage says: 'comment is free but facts are sacred'. Yet while the British press is free to support particular political parties and policies, broadcasters are legally required to abstain from editorial comment and taking sides. Not only must they give a factually accurate account of the news, they are also bound to balance different opinions and arguments from the mainstream of British life in matters of major controversy. In other words, broadcasters must be objective and impartial. The reporting of race suggests they are neither.

Industrial Relations: 'Bad News' from the Glasgow University Media Group

Industrial relations is an area where there are deep conflicts of interest over jobs, pay and working conditions. How an industrial dispute is reported will be a question of great concern to managers and workers alike. An ideological account of a dispute as the fault of one group may prejudice the way in which it is resolved, especially by influencing public opinion. Moreover, representations of workers and managers in the reporting of industrial relations in general may adversely affect their public credibility; for example, images of trade unions as greedy and selfish may undermine the legitimacy of strike action.

Amongst the most famous (some would say notorious) recent studies of media representations has been the work of the Glasgow University Media Group on industrial relations. It has been particularly controversial amongst broadcasters themselves because it challenges their claim to be impartial and objective. This section examines their research.

The Group's first book *Bad News* (1976) was concerned with television coverage of industrial relations in 1975. They found that reports of strikes and disputes concentrated unduly on certain specific industries at the expense of others. As a whole there was 'no consistent relationship between the stoppages recorded during the first five months of 1975 and those reported by television news' (p. 167). The motor vehicle industry was singled out, while other industries like shipbuilding or engineering received little attention. For example, engineering, which had well over twice as many stoppages as the motor vehicle industry, involving roughly the same number of workers and accounting for about a quarter of working days lost in *all* industries, appeared in only two news stories. In the case of one car manufacturer, British Leyland, news broadcasts frequently mentioned strikes as the key problem facing the company, despite the fact that the government-sponsored Ryder Report rejected the view that they were the major difficulty in BL and blamed lack of investment and management failings. In one example the Glasgow Group show that a speech by the then Prime Minister, Harold Wilson, which criticised both management and unions was edited in such a way as to sound like a criticism of the workforce only. However, whereas the BBC began by reporting the criticisms that had been made of both groups, later narrowing this down to only one of them, ITN completely failed to acknowledge Wilson's criticisms of management, portraying the speech as 'a blunt warning' to workers. Generally speaking, disputes were reported in terms of 'trouble' and inconvenience, as in this statement from a BBC2 news review:

> The week had its share of unrest. Trouble in Glasgow with striking dustmen and ambulance controllers, short time in the car industry, no *Sunday Mirror* or *Sunday People* today and a fair amount of general trouble in Fleet Street and a continuing rumble over the matter of two builders' pickets jailed for conspiracy (p. 23).

The authors conclude that 'viewers were given a misleading portrayal of industrial disputes in the UK when measured against the independent reality of events'. At the same time, other industrial matters such as accidents at work are considerably under-reported and usually only appear when linked to disaster stories, even though they account for many working days being lost.

A second book, appropriately called *More Bad News* (1980), continues this work and argues that there is a uniformity or 'lack of competitiveness' in broadcast news. The Group details a slanting in the presentation of arguments so that some points of view fail to gain a proper hearing. For example, in a case study of the reporting of economic affairs in 1975 the authors show that wage inflation was the dominant explanation given of the nation's problems. This was a matter of the sheer weighting given to this theme which occurred in 383 references between January–April 1975. Investment was mentioned only 89 times in spite of its importance. For example, the ITN industrial correspondent stated that 'since the war, Britain's overriding problem, almost universally agreed, has been a failure to invest adequately' (p. 24). Similarly, the language applied to industrial disputes in news broadcasts was found to be heavily stereotyped, using warlike imagery and describing workers as nearly always making 'claims' or 'demands', while employers 'offer' or 'propose'. By contrast, sentences like 'management demand higher output' rarely appeared. Language is especially significant since news film is merely used for illustration and the bulk of news consists of talk or what are known in the trade as 'talking heads' – typified by the news reader. Thus in TV news written or spoken story lines predominate over visuals. Interviews were often prejudicial, especially where these were filmed outside the TV studio. In the reporting of industrial disputes management was typically interviewed in an office and asked about the consequences of the dispute for their firm or organisation, while workers were interviewed outdoors – on pickets or after mass meetings – and asked for an explanation or justification of their position, rather than about the problems the dispute created for them. Interviews of this kind have an *agenda-setting* role – they fix and thereby limit the terms in which an issue will be thought through and discussed. Not surprisingly recent TUC guidelines have warned union representatives to avoid interviews which are structured in this manner, noting that 'a background of a busy street or factory gate with on-lookers peering over your shoulder will not help if you have a complicated case to explain'. The Glasgow Media Group conclude that broadcasters 'continually reinforce a managerially skewed view of industrial relations' (p. 189).

This research is not without its critics. One difficulty is that the authors are often relying on case studies to make their point, and this means that their evidence can be rather sketchy. For instance, as Philip Elliott (1981) has observed, their argument that the use of super-captions to identify interviewees is discriminatory (so that 'lower case is lower class') is based on just two examples taken from one sample week's broadcasting. A more damaging criticism is that the Glasgow Group have failed to see that it is not impartiality but 'due impartiality' which broadcasters have to achieve. As Tony Bennett has pointed out 'due impartiality' entails recognising 'not just the whole range of views on an issue', but also 'the weights of opinion which hold these views' (Bennett, 1982b, p. 306). In other words, it is perfectly acceptable for broadcasters to give more attention to some views than to others if they believe that these carry wider support in society. We should not be surprised if broadcasters reflect the status quo – this is what 'due impartiality' requires them to do. To suggest that there could be an absolute impartiality on our screens is to misunderstand what broadcasting in our society is really about.

Another criticism which has been levelled at the Glasgow Media Group is that their work is fairly strong on description, but weak on explanation. While it shows us that distortions do occur in the media, that these are far from being random and have a discernible pattern to them, it does not give us a very good account of why this happens. Philip Elliott has argued that the Glasgow Group ultimately put the bias they detect down to the 'conscious product of broadcasting élites' – that is to say, they adopt a conspiracy theory in which bias is deliberate, as if TV were directly manipulated on behalf of the more powerful members of society. This criticism is not entirely fair, but it does have a grain of truth in it. The Glasgow Group do emphasise the importance of the self-conscious or 'reflexive' role of senior managers in broadcasting who enjoy real power within their institutions, backing this up with evidence from the minutes of top boardroom meetings which have been leaked to them. Yet the authors also note that much of the time broadcasters' tacitly trade upon the unspoken and dominant ideology of our society', uncritically accepting received ideas which favour those who own and control business. However, the relationship between deliberate and unwitting types of bias is not explained and we do not really learn how and why bias occurs.

So far we have looked at representations of gender, race and industrial relations and asked whether the media present a misleading or ideological view of their place in society. The remainder of this chapter deals with a fourth topic which figures prominently in the media – that of crime. A final part reviews some problems with the claim that media representations are ideological.

The Reporting of Crime

Much of our knowledge of the everyday occurrence of crime comes from reading newspapers. In fact, the press has a near monopoly on this kind of information. But how accurate is this knowledge? Jason Ditton and James Duffy (1983) investigated the reporting of crime in six Scottish newspapers during the month of March 1981. Their analysis focussed particularly upon the Strathclyde region which has the largest number of reported crimes committed in Scotland. The press here has a very high readership with most people reading at least one newspaper per day. Yet this major source of information about crime was found to give a very inaccurate picture.

Ditton and Duffy calculated the amount of space in each paper which was devoted to crime news and also the percentage of this which dealt with Scottish crime news and crime which specifically related to the Strathclyde area. They found that the reporting of crime was only a small percentage of news coverage as a whole, making up on average 6.5% of all news, of which over a quarter was regional crime news. Although the amount of space given over to crime might not appear to be very great, it was the major source of images of crime in the locality. What was especially striking was the highly selective nature of the press reports. When compared with the regional crime statistics for the period in question less than 1% of crimes made known to the police or brought to court appeared in the newspapers. This would be defensible if the categories of crime covered in the press fairly reflected the actual incidence of crime in the region. However, Ditton and Duffy uncovered a very marked pattern of biased coverage where crimes involved sex or violence. Crimes of violence that had been made known to the police were over-reported in the papers by 19.4 times their actual occurrence, and crimes involving indecency were over-reported by 8.1 times. Similarly, violent crimes dealt with in court were over-reported by 36.2 times their real number, and crimes of indecency were over-reported by 34.3 times. At the same time, motoring offences, which accounted for over 40% of all court cases, received hardly any coverage at all.

Ditton and Duffy suggest that this kind of sensational reporting which uses scare-mongering headlines like 'ARMED BANDITS TAKE TO THE STREETS' greatly inflates people's fears of crime, particularly amongst vulnerable groups like the old. In fact this has the cultural effect of misinforming the public by a deceptive emphasis on those crimes which are relatively untypical of crime as a whole with the result 'that people's growing anxiety about crime is not commensurate with increases in crime itself' (Ditton & Duffy, 1983, p. 164).

A Marxist Perspective on Crime Reporting: The Case of Mugging

For Marxists law and order has to be understood as part of the class struggle. Marx believed that the increasingly severe crises stemming from the problems faced by the economic system would intensify class conflict between the proletariat or working class and the bourgeoisie or ruling class. On the one hand, Marx argued that this would bring members of the proletariat to organise themselves politically as they came to recognise their common interests, and their struggles would lead to a new kind of society in which classes and class privilege were a thing of the past. However, he also suggested that this process might be held back by the power of ruling class ideas in society as a whole. This was his theory of ideology. It stated that the ideas which were dominant in any historical period would always be those of the ruling class. This was not a matter of deliberately hoodwinking people; rather, the bourgeoisie would naturally expect other social classes to view society in the same way that they did and had the power and influence to promote this kind of thinking. For example, the law, in defending private property, the basis of the class structure, is both coercive and ideological, since 'laws enacted according to the dictates of a dominant ideology will appear to the members of that society as rules designed to preserve the natural social and economic order' (Collins, 1982, p. 43).

Policing the Crisis (1978) by Stuart Hall *et al* looks at the role of the media in promoting ideological representations of law and order. The authors skilfully combine labelling theory with Marxist political economy in an investigation of the moral panic surrounding the controversial crime of 'mugging' in Britain in the early 1970s. They suggest that it marked an important change in the manner in which the ruling class was able to exercise power in society, a change aided by the media.

Their explanation of what happened draws upon the work of the Italian Marxist Antonio Gramsci. Gramsci used the term 'hegemony' to emphasise that the ruling class does not merely rule, it *leads* – in other words, the bourgeoisie maintains power by persuading other classes in society to give their consent to its aims and policies. This power is both moral and intellectual – it convinces people that ruling class views are right and thus wins public arguments – and this enables it to mobilise the support of those it governs. Gramsci's concept is valuable, Hall and his associates claim, because it extends our understanding of what ideology really means in a practical sense. Using this concept they argue that by the late 1960s Britain was experiencing a crisis of hegemony in which its ruling class was finding it increasingly hard to hold on to the consent of the populace. The causes of this crisis were ultimately economic, rooted in the beginnings of the end of the successful post-war industrial boom. This had been successful not simply because it 'delivered the goods' of material prosperity – it had also brought with it an ideology of affluence and consumption, illustrated by the claim that a process of 'embourgeoisement' was taking place whereby many manual workers were adopting the values and life-style of the middle class. At the same time ruling class hegemony rested on a political consensus in which the opposing parties tended to concur in the view that the fundamental problems facing modern industrial societies had been solved and that all that was needed now were minor adjustments. Once these ideas became harder to believe as economic realities started to call them into question a new foundation for social order had to be found.

As a response to this crisis the ruling class was forced to become more coercive by strengthening the police, the courts and the law – for example, the attempt to control strikes and industrial disputes through new legislation. In ideological terms this meant that 'law and order' became a central theme of political debate. It served as a way of winning people over to the view that a stronger State was needed. Hall and his associates suggest that mugging became especially important as a symbol of the fear of a disordered, troubled society, and that the media had a crucial role in creating and sustaining this image, an image that brought together social anxieties focussed around youth, race and crime.

It is important to bear in mind that in strictly legal terms the crime of 'mugging' does not exist. As a label for crime it is an American import which only began to appear in the British press in the late 1960s in stories of urban breakdown in cities like New York, sometimes with the implication that it was soon destined to spread to England. The first report of a specifically English mugging occurred in August 1972 when a murder near Waterloo station was described by a policeman as 'a mugging gone wrong'. However, its uncertain legal status made it a term that was often difficult to apply. For example, when the Home Secretary wrote to police chiefs at the height of the scare asking for more statistical information he offered a definition of the crime which even the police found confusing. A senior officer in Southampton wrote in reply that it was 'very difficult to differentiate mugging from the old traditional crime of a seaman getting "rolled" ' (Hall *et al*, 1978, p. 5). In fact most muggings were charged as 'robberies' or 'assaults with intent to rob', well-known criminal charges covering a wide variety of circumstances. Statistics relating to mugging have always been highly contentious.

Hall and his associates suggest that if we compare the figures for 'robbery or assault with intent to rob' between 1955–1965 with those between 1965–1972 the rate of increase had fallen by well over two-thirds. Despite this, even before mugging had begun to surface as a 'new' social problem in the courts and the media, there is evidence of an increase in police activity with the setting up of special squads to deal with urban crime. This was a strengthening of the 'control culture' which actually anticipated what was to follow. Mugging was one of many themes by which the State justified its already increasingly coercive stance. This is not to deny that street crime was a problem, but it is to suggest that its significance was over-rated and its portrayal extremely misleading.

The role of the press in this process of exaggeration was vital, because of its subordinate relationship to the main centres of power in society. For reasons that will be discussed more fully in the next chapter newspapers are unusually dependent upon the police as a source of information. The police are accredited with expert status and are among those who have special access to the media. As a result the media naturally tend 'to reproduce symbolically the existing structure of power in society's institutional order' (p. 58). However, newspapers are not simply mouthpieces of the ruling class: the press takes the 'primary interpretations' with which it has been provided and turns them into items of news according to the norms and values which make up the journalists' professional culture. Stories are translated into the particular stylised version of everyday language in which each paper addresses its public. In this way the press claims to speak on its readers' behalf and at the same time its statements serve to confirm the policies and actions of the control culture so that each supports the other, a process Hall *et al* call 'taking the public voice' (p. 63). The rhetoric of police statements and courtroom verdicts is passed back and forth by the press and this focusses and channels popular opinion. The press supplies the link between those in the control culture who define and deal with social problems and the public.

Once set in motion newspaper reporting has its own rhythms and news stories follow a logic peculiar to themselves. Mugging started off as something extraordinary, what the *Daily Mirror* called 'a frightening new strain of crime'. The newness of the label was what made it frightening, for as we have seen it was arguably not new at all. Press coverage of mugging peaked in October 1972 and then began to go into decline. By August of the following year one 'cycle of newsworthiness' was over. The supposed novelty of the crime was no longer enough to keep it in the limelight. After this new twists had to be found to keep the story alive, and these usually took the form of bizarre or humorous news angles, such as that of a youth forcing 'a man, who had no money, into a bank at knife-point in order to cash a cheque' (pp. 70–4). When the next cycle of newsworthiness began in 1975 mugging was specifically identified with West Indian youth and linked to the continuing tensions between the police and the black community in areas like Lambeth and Brixton. Each news cycle presents us with a set of 'facts', and puts them into a context so that they make sense. Hall and his associates wish to dispute both the facts and the context that the press have supplied about mugging. They argue that the press helped to create a moral panic, an ideological over-reaction which served ruling class interests at a time of crisis.

Their analysis raises a number of questions. Hall and his associates may be criticised for failing to make clear why mugging was so important to the crisis they discuss – in other words, how did the image of mugging particularly come to represent the experience of social upheaval at the time that it did? Was it really a prior economic and political crisis which made it so important *ideologically*, or are other explanations possible? For example, the scepticism which the authors display towards the mugging statistics makes the relationship between the problem of crime, changes in policing, and the reports in the press seem very uncertain, especially since they insist that ' "mugging" *was* a real social and historical event arising out of its own kind of struggle' (p. 186). As John Lea and Jock Young (1982) have argued, (citing *Policing the Crisis* in support), 'the inner city crime rate is extremely high' and racial discrimination and urban deprivation 'sets the scene for the development of a vicious circle whereby relations between police and community deteriorate in such a way that each step in deterioration creates pressure for further deterioration'. If we could clarify the causal links involved here we might well have to re-evaluate our view of the role of the press.

Crime in Fiction: Thrillers

Many of our representations of crime come to us through media fictions of all kinds. These have always been extremely popular; for example, a survey of viewing habits amongst *Sunday Times* readers carried out in October 1982 revealed that 'mysteries' were still the type of film that most people preferred watching on TV. Thrillers like the James Bond novels sell in their millions. They contain a distinctive view of the world which feeds into the reader's enjoyment of these books.

Jerry Palmer in his book *Thrillers* (1979) has tried to find out what it is about narratives like these that grip us so compulsively and why they came to prominence in the modern period. First of all, he picks out the unique formula which distinguish thrillers from other genres, and make them a special kind of fictional experience. Palmer mainly discusses literary texts, but his analysis could also be applied to film or TV. He argues that thrillers are always built around two common elements which are closely interlinked: the hero and the conspiracy. This means that the same formula actually underpins a wide range of texts including Agatha Christie's classically English detective stories, tough-guy private eye novels by Raymond Chandler and Mickey Spillane and the spy thrillers of Ian Fleming and John le Carré. In all these books what sets the story in motion is 'a mysterious con- spiracy . . . that springs from nowhere, which produces events whose source is incomprehensible' (p. 86). The task of the hero is to unravel the mystery and so avert the conspiracy; indeed the hero is the only person with the special qualities it takes to do this. If this is the heart of the story, then everything else is, strictly speaking, secondary to it – for example, the sexual encounters in the James Bond novels are there merely to underline his status as hero and this is why women are portrayed in a stereotyped way. But such encounters are not essential to the thriller. The Sherlock Holmes stories contain few references to sexuality at all. Here the hero's status emerges through the contrast with his muddled assistant Dr. Watson or the bumbling Inspector Lestrade.

The addictive pleasure of the thriller results from our identifying with the hero as the sole point of certainty in a world that is under threat, at least for the duration of the story. Thus our 'excitement and suspense derive from wholeheartedly wanting one person to succeed and fearing setbacks to their projects' (p. 62). Once the conspiracy is under way nothing is what it seems, and this is just as true when it is the identity of the villain which is at the root of the mystery, as in an Agatha Christie novel, or when the villain's identity is known but the nature of his or her plan is not, as in most James Bond stories. Palmer's claim is that no other popular genres work quite like this, even where they make use of mystery and suspense as an added ingredient. For example, romantic love stories have heroes and heroines but their plots are dominated by the quest for happiness, and where mysteries do occur, they are only one of many possible barriers to a happy ending.

Palmer argues that the emergence of the twin elements of hero and conspiracy can be traced back to changes in ideology during the industrial revolution. Although heroism as an ideal goes back to feudal times, its modern form is the embodiment of competitive individualism. The hero is set apart from society in the thriller – so much so that ordinary laws may not apply to him. James Bond, for example, is specially 'licensed to kill'. Thus he is an exceptional individual in a male-dominated society which is represented as a collection of individuals, who constantly have to compete with each other in order to be successful and so prove themselves. This ideology legitimates the competitive behaviour required by a society which is based on the economy of the market. The hero is the successful competitor writ large. The theme of conspiracy, on the other hand, derives from a shift in attitudes to law and order in which crimes against property and crimes against the person came to be seen as the same kind of threat to the social order. This change reflected the growing importance of private property in the nineteenth century. The first thrillers therefore coincided with the founding of the modern police force, and put forward 'a paranoid representation of the world' (p. 86).

Because of the nature of this ideology, Palmer tends to see the thriller as an intrinsically conservative genre. In the thriller 'courageous intervention by one man . . . saves the Western way of life' (p. 205). This description fits the James Bond novels, but whether it can be applied to the whole range of texts that Palmer wishes to explain is more doubtful. Palmer's strict classification does not help us to understand, for example, how the Bond films evolved into the technological spectaculars they are today, nor the tie-in between the films and the books which have clearly influenced the popularity of both. As Tony Bennett has pointed out, following the first Bond film in 1961 sales of the novels in Britain rose from 300,000 the previous year to a peak of nearly 7 million in 1965. He concludes that 'for the vast majority of readers, the films . . . must be taken into account in assessing their relationship to and mode of reading the novels' (Bennett, 1982a, p. 11). A further weakness is that Palmer's stress on the conservative slant of the genre fails to account for the variety shown by thrillers: Joseph Hansen's novels, for example, consciously aim to offer positive representations of homosexual self-identity and life-style by portraying a gay detective hero. This suggests that some thrillers may use the techniques of popular writing to challenge rather than support the status quo.

The remaining sections in this chapter discuss some criticisms of the idea that the mass media promote stereotyping and ideology.

Anderson and Sharrock – An Ethnomethodological Critique of Media Studies

Some writers have been extremely sceptical of many of the analyses of news and current affairs which have been discussed in this chapter. Anderson and Sharrock (1979) base their criticisms on an ethnomethodological perspective. Ethnomethodologists argue that the main feature of social life is that it consists of orderly interaction between the members of society and that this follows unacknowledged or taken-for-granted rules. For example, ethnomethodologists have investigated the rules which make ordinary conversations possible, like those which ensure that we take regular turns when speaking to one another. Flouting such rules can bring interaction to an abrupt halt. Researchers in this tradition have been particularly interested in the use of language in the achievement of social order.

Anderson and Sharrock re-analysed a study by Graham Murdock in which he used a random selection of news stories from his local paper, the *Leicester Mercury,* to show how the press promoted ideological images of young people. Murdock argued that news stories about youth rely on two contrasting stereotypes embodied in sensational headlines: well-adjusted high-achievers – as in the headline 'BOY, 16, SWIMS THE CHANNEL' – and unruly, anti-social delinquents – as in 'YOUTH THREATENED WITH KNIFE AS GANG GO ON RAMPAGE'. These stereotypes are, according to Murdock 'typical of the routine news coverage of young people'. They exacerbate popular fears of youth whilst hiding their root causes which lie in social deprivation.

Anderson and Sharrock find this line of argument unsatisfactory because it misunderstands the implicit rules by which we read headlines in general and these headlines in particular. They claim that Murdock takes the headlines out of the practical context of reading and neglects the cues and skills that go into making sense of them; by doing so he makes readers out to be more gullible and less discerning than they really are. In any newspaper, Anderson and Sharrock suggest, headlines merely perform the task of arousing a reader's curiosity and pointing to the sort of story we are about to read – one of a series, a story with a moral, or perhaps a piece of comment. Put simply, a headline serves as a preface or signpost which directs attention to a particular story: it tells the reader what to expect, not what to believe. In the case of the boy channel-swimmer the headline announces an extraordinary and unlikely achievement in just the same way as would a headline like 'MAN WHO ONLY LEARNED TO SWIM LAST YEAR SWIMS CHANNEL' or 'EIGHTY YEAR OLD SWIMS CHANNEL'. It makes no generalisation about contemporary youth at all, contrary to Murdock's claims – 'it is Murdock that stereotypes youth not the local newspaper'. Similarly the 'rampage' headline arouses only a sense of drama and danger in the reader's locality – notice that the gang that is mentioned is not itself described as young. Whereas Murdock argues that dramatic headlines encourage ideological thought, Anderson and Sharrock suggest that they are nothing more than cues devised to guide the reader round a newspaper. These cues assist in the task of reading, but need not influence our beliefs.

In reply Murdock (1980) has cited the interviews he carried out with the parents of teenagers as evidence that the press stereotypes he has identified do influence public perceptions of young people. However, for Anderson and Sharrock this is no answer at all since they see Murdock's questions to parents as being based upon careless and unjustifiable readings of newspaper materials and therefore only too likely to confirm Murdock's own theoretical point of view by eliciting the answers he wants to hear. In summary, Anderson and Sharrock would not accept that news headlines have the ideological content it is sometimes said they do. They argue not only for greater care in the analysis of media output but also for the adoption of a new perspective – ethnomethodology. This viewpoint stresses the importance of understanding how audiences actually go about reading what is in the media. Anderson and Sharrock claim that in this case the audience – readers of the *Leicester Mercury* – use headlines as cues, guidelines and ways of making sense of newspaper content. By contrast, the so-called ideological component is really only the researcher's way of making sense of media output. One is imposing one's views upon the audience by suggesting that ideological messages are reaching newspaper readers. Anderson and Sharrock argue that such researchers have failed to discover the way readers use and make sense of newspaper headlines and media output in general.

The Problem of Ideology

Many of the studies reviewed in this chapter have used the concept of ideology critically to show that media representations serve powerful vested interests in society. The strongest version of this approach comes from the Marxist perspective which argues that there is a dominant ideology which supports the capitalist ruling class and that this is associated with its control over the means of mental production. However, the notion of a dominant ideology which somehow draws together different representations of society into a seamless web of domination is one that is fraught with difficulties.

Abercrombie, Hill and Turner (1980) have challenged the idea that there is a clearly identifiable ideology in the later stages of capitalism. They argue that business enterprises now rely much less upon the inheritance of family capital since this has been replaced by impersonal financial institutions like pension funds. As a result, the traditional ideology of property developed during earlier phases of capitalism has been weakened and it is doubtful whether any new dominant ideology has taken its place. The status quo is now secured by such factors as the mutual interdependence between different sections of the division of labour, increased material benefits enjoyed by many employees, the economic compulsion of daily work, and the threat of physical force wielded by those who hold power. Ironically, this process of ideological decline is argued to have occurred at the same time as the means of transmitting ideology have become exceptionally efficient, particularly with the growth of the modern mass media. Thus, although the media is potentially a powerful tool of domination, it lacks a central ideological vision, because ideology is not as important as it once was. Against this argument, the studies discussed in this chapter tend to suggest that media representations often present an ideological picture of people and events, which seriously distorts the knowledge which we have of them. Nevertheless, Abercrombie, Hill and Turner's work has raised an interesting and difficult question: how far do representations like these add up to a single ideological viewpoint which significantly contributes to the integration of modern societies? The authors query the assumption that the media 'do disseminate a coherent set of values which derive from a dominant ideology' (p. 130).

This chapter has considered the images and representations found in the mass media and the part they play in social life. Sometimes, as in the case of certain representations of women, they may be a source of enjoyment and pleasure, helping to define a group's view of itself. However, where representations are stereotyped they can also be a source of ideology: individuals and social situations are depicted in such a way as to confer power on some groups and deny it to others. To look at who is being represented in the media and how they are being represented is to gain a unique insight into the nature of power and conflict in contemporary society.

Chapter Three

The Structure and Organisation of the Mass Media

The previous chapter examined the images and representations found in the mass media and showed that their treatment of such topics as crime, race or gender tend to fall into recurring patterns. These contribute to our view of the social world, and are likely to be particularly influential where other sources of information are lacking – that is, they may have a cultural effect. Many writers would argue that the media help create an ideological climate which disguises the true character of society and disadvantages some social groups against others. However, we have yet to really tackle the difficult question of why these distortions occur. To do this we will need to examine how the media are organised and the kind of work that people in the media do. As Janet Wolff has argued, 'ideological analysis is insufficient if it is not supplemented by an understanding of groups, pressures, hierarchies and power relations within organisations involved in the general process of the production of culture' (Wolff, 1981, pp. 30–1).

In trying to explain the patterning of stories and images, sociologists have generally tried to avoid two equally simplistic answers. The first of these suggests that the patterns we find in the media are the result of a conspiracy, a deliberate attempt to mislead or misrepresent. Some versions of Marxism find this idea of the media as a manipulative expression of ruling class interests attractive. The difficulty with this view is that it is hard to demonstrate. It is one thing to show that some members of society consistently have greater power, opportunity and advantage than others, but quite another to prove that, say, a particular story in a newspaper is the consequence of a small tightly-knit group seeking to exercise control over the rest of us. The second answer views media output solely as a response to audience demand. However, while sales and audiences are clearly vital to the media's survival, this argument ignores the way in which the media are organised to meet, encourage and even shape that demand, and also the work that goes into making what are very stylised products. The first section of this chapter examines the question of the ownership and control of the mass media and its relation to the range of products they make available to us.

Ownership and Control in the Mass Media

One of the major trends in industry this century has been the growth of the large business corporation. Media industries are no exception to this, but it is important to bear in mind that government intervention into radio and television has meant that the shape taken by some media organisations has been influenced by considerations of national policy rather than purely commercial criteria. Even with a recent willingness to leave the media more open to market forces than before, the problem of a communications monopoly arising amongst some sections of private enterprise is still taken sufficiently seriously to warrant traditional restrictions on new developments. Thus in July 1983 the Department of Trade announced that existing local newspaper, radio and television companies would not be permitted to own or have a controlling interest (i.e. owning more than 50% of shares) in cable television companies in their own areas (*Guardian*, 19.7.83). Nevertheless, as the next section shows, the mass media are big business.

Concentration and Conglomeration

A very high percentage of what we see, hear and read during our leisure derives from a small number of extremely large companies. At least two-thirds of the British audience for daily and Sunday newspapers, paperbacks, records and commercial TV programmes are served by the top five firms dealing in these products. This domination of the market is even more striking in other media. When you visit the local cinema or buy a woman's magazine, the chances are that in each case your money will be going to one of the top two companies in that field. For instance, since the early 1940s cinema chains have been in the hands of a duopoly: Rank and Associated British Cinemas (ABC). These are only the most dramatic examples of a process that has been at work throughout the media, that of *concentration*. Concentration refers to firms in the same line of business merging with one another.

A second process which has been changing the structure and organisation of firms is potentially more significant still. The term *con-*

glomeration is used to refer to firms with different business interests coming together to form new giant corporations. There are two main forms this can take. *General conglomerates* are the result of a takeover of a company specialising in one or more branches of the mass media by another with non-media industrial or commercial interests. A case in point was the takeover of *The Observer* by the Lonrho Group in February 1981 in a £6 million deal. In such cases there may be public concern that a decline in quality will occur because the newly acquired company will be submerged in the industrial identity of the parent conglomerate. These feelings can be exacerbated by the speed and stealth with which business mergers are conducted, and the rapid changes in management which often follow. The assumption behind such fears is that the media are not like other industries and cannot be run along the same lines, an assumption which finds support in the professional self-image of media personnel.

Multi-media or *communications conglomerates* occur where companies operating almost exclusively within media or leisure industries merge. The takeover of Times Newspapers by Rupert Murdoch's News International is a good example of this. Murdoch's company also owns the *Sun* and the *News of the World* and has annual profits of around £25 million. His other business interests include Australian television and aviation firms as well as an international chain of newspapers. To take only the United States, Murdoch's News America Publishing Inc., jointly owned by News Limited of Australia and News International Ltd. of Britain, controls the *New York Post*, the *Village Voice* and *New York Magazine* and also a number of newspapers and magazines in Texas. Conglomerates often have world-wide business interests. For example, the bulk of records sold throughout the world are produced by four huge multi-national companies – two of these are American-based (CBS and WEA), while the remaining two are European (EMI and Polygram).

Many conglomerates have deliberately pursued a policy of diversification, collecting together a very varied portfolio of business interests in order to compensate for possible losses in any one field of activity. The Rank Organization met the long-term decline in cinema attendance by branching out into hotels, television and hi-fi equipment and motorway services. The Granada Group is another example of this strategy and includes cinema, bingo clubs, motorway services, music publishing and the second largest television rental chain. It was formerly Britain's fourth largest paperback publishing company (owning Panther, Paladin and Mayflower books) – although book sales never provided more than 2% of the group's total profits between 1978–83. However, in March 1983 these publishing interests were bought up by William Collins Ltd. (owners of Fontana paperbacks) in a deal which pushed that company into neck-and-neck rivalry with Pearson Longman, the publishers of Penguin books, each jointly leading the UK publishing industry with about 25% of the paperback market each. Interestingly, Collins had successfully fought off a take-over bid by Murdoch's News International Ltd. in 1981 in which Murdoch had acquired a 42.3% share in their company.

Events like these vividly illustrate the fast-moving world of takeovers and mergers. What has happened to the mass media is only one instance of a wider set of changes in corporate structure and organisation which have been gathering speed since the mid-1950s. Between 1957 and 1968 nearly 40% of all the companies with shares listed on the London Stock Exchange were swallowed up in mergers and acquisitions, and from 1967 to 1973 the number of mergers among manufacturing and commercial companies rose from 1,709 to 2,415 (Murdock, 1982, p. 119).

The Debate about Corporate Control

The sheer scale of these conglomerates obviously raises questions about the economic power which they wield. The idea that property would become concentrated in fewer and fewer hands and that society would polarize into two classes – those who own the means of production and those who have only their ability to work as a way of making a living – is, of course, associated with Karl Marx. Latter day radical writers have used the kind of evidence outlined above as proof that Marx's key predictions have been vindicated by history. At the same time, others have argued that modern industry is different from anything that Marx envisaged, and that these dissimilarities show Marx to have been wrong. Since the mass media are, in Ralph Miliband's words, 'not only business, but big business' we need to see what this debate is about (Miliband, 1973, p. 203).

Critics of Marx have argued that his account of social class was based upon capitalist private enterprise at only one stage of its development. He saw the capitalist as an entrepreneur who both owned and ran his company, and power resided in a privileged class of propertied families. However, the second half of the nineteenth century saw the family firm begin to change into the joint-stock company, or what would today be called the corporation. This was simply a way of expanding the activities of the firm by raising money from the sale of shares to outside investors, and in the last hundred years it has become 'the dominant feature of the economic landscape' (Scott, 1979, p. 15).

Writers like Ralf Dahrendorf have argued that this has resulted in the break-up of the ruling class as Marx understood it. There are two reasons for this. Firstly, with the sale of shares, ownership of the firm ceases to lie with the individual entrepreneur and belongs to the body of shareholders, each of whose shares carries with it a vote in electing the board of directors. More than this, it was claimed that as shares were made as widely available as possible in the search for capital, so share ownership would become increasingly fragmented. Some writers, like Adolf Berle, have even suggested that the outcome would be a 'people's capitalism' in which everyone would have a stake. Secondly, the decline of the owner-entrepreneur who had actively managed his own company, together with the increasing size of the corporation, meant that a new group of professional managers came to the fore, and it was they who really ran the industrial system. In short, ownership had become separated from control and a 'managerial revolution' was in progress in which managers were becoming a new ruling élite. Their professional expertise and their privileged access to corporate information allowed them to outflank the shareholders, depriving them of their power and leaving them little option but to approve the decisions the managers had already made. Indeed, the distancing of owners from managers opened up the possibility that the latter would develop a new approach to business, one less interested in profit-making for its own sake and more concerned with the social respon- sibilities of their work.

Defenders of Marx point out that in actual fact he was well aware of the new importance of the joint-stock company. In *Capital Vol. III* he also noted that it had 'the tendency to separate this function of managerial work more and more from the possession of capital'. His view was that the manager was only a 'mere manager', a functionary working for the capitalist, and the salary the manager received was 'simply the wage for a certain kind of skilled labour' (Marx, 1981, pp. 512 & 567). The capitalist class had not been dissolved because of the spread of share-ownership, nor was it being replaced by a new managerial élite.

Having sketched in an outline of this controversy, I now want to see how it relates to a specific example in the mass media: the British press.

Power and Influence in the British Press

We have already seen some evidence of concentration in the British newspaper industry in the discussion of multi-media conglomerates. Who controls the press is a crucial issue in a society which values freedom of speech. Journalists often like to present themselves as public watchdogs protecting us from the abuses of power. But how do these cherished values and ideals square with the facts about the corporate structure of the British press?

Graham Murdock (1980) suggests that sociological work on the newspaper industry has tended to divide into two camps. On the one side there are the pluralist defenders of the press who argue that it is truly independent; while on the other side stand the radical critics who follow Marx in believing that 'the class which has the means of production at its disposal, has control at the same time over the means of mental production' and is able to 'regulate the production and distribution of the ideas of their age' (Marx and Engels, 1966, pp. 64–5). Broadly speaking, then, these two different positions reflect the wider debate about the significance of changing patterns of ownership and control.

Pluralists argue that power in society is dispersed amongst a variety of interest groups which do not coincide with the property relations discussed by Marx. According to adherents of this perspective, 'pluralistic societies are dotted with a variety of pressure groups, some of them striving to promote more or less overtly political aims' (Gurevitch and Blumler, 1977, p. 286). Free competition between firms is often cited in support of this argument. For example, across the different branches of the British media some 25 companies vie for market domination (see Tunstall, 1983, p. 174). Not only is this dispersal of power true of society as a whole, it is also a feature of the communities and organisations within it, so that it is hard for any one group to gain the upper hand for long. The separation of ownership and control is just one special instance of this general principle. There is, however, one institution which does threaten the independence of the various groupings in society and that is the State, which has an unrivalled monopoly of power and may at times fail to be the servant of the people. This pluralist view finds much favour in Fleet Street and is regularly put forward by newspaper representatives. Their belief is that owners' desires for profit, editors' and journalists' professional interests and the demands of their readers are all finely balanced. Thus, according to journalist John Whale, the power of the proprietors 'where it survives at all . . . must still defer to the influence of readers' (Whale, 1977, p. 84).

The radical and Marxist opponents of this position have criticised it from two different angles. Graham Murdock labels these 'instrumentalist' versus 'structuralist' approaches. Where they differ is in the attention they give to particular aspects of the way in which corporations operate. For instrumentalists the key question for research to establish is: 'Who holds power and how is it exercised?' Structuralists, on the other hand, are more concerned with showing how the policies pursued by the corporations stem from their place in the capitalist system and follow its economic logic. Each of these approaches will now be examined in turn.

Instrumentalists like Ralph Miliband argue that the facts about concentration and conglomeration undermine the pluralist case. Far from there being a divorce between ownership and control, ultimate power resides with the owners who are effectively able to determine long-term policies such as whether to expand or invest, whether to close or to merge, and who also decide on the hiring and firing of executives. Managers only have discretion within the framework set by such policies or decisions and therefore have only a limited form of control, sometimes described as 'operational control'. It is not difficult to show that a few large companies dominate the market. 85% of the circulation of all daily and Sunday papers, whether local or national, is covered by seven major newspaper publishers. These are among the biggest companies in the British economy, with four included in the top 150 corporations and the other three in the top 500. There has also been a marked move towards diversification since the mid-1950s, and the majority now have extensive interests elsewhere in the media, most notably in book publishing and commercial television. Instead of this leading to a more dispersed form of ownership, however, 'in five out of seven leading concerns, the controlling interests remain in the hands of the original founding families and their associates', families such as the Harmsworths and the Berrys (Murdock, 1980, p. 45). Instrumentalists argue that these owners share the same social background and participate in a common way of life: they can be identified as typical members of a privileged ruling class, bending the running of the corporations to their own designs. Even where the press is run by relative outsiders like the Canadian Lord Thomson and Australian Rupert Murdoch, it is still the case that they have benefitted from an Oxbridge university education. A top public school education, followed by Oxford or Cambridge, and membership of exclusive London clubs like Whites or the Royal Yacht binds such men together into a cohesive social group and links them to their fellows elsewhere in industry and the City. This is further reinforced by the overlap between companies that occurs through interlocking directorships so that the same individuals will sit on several different boards of directors giving them opportunities for sharing business information and access to channels of influence. It is this combination of shared life-style and boardroom experience that makes newspaper owners part of a capitalist class and therefore we should not be surprised at the one-sidedness of the press and its support for this class.

Structuralists claim that this sort of argument gives us a misleading picture of the press as nothing more than a tool (or instrument) of the capitalist ruling class and that its emphasis on personal decisions and group membership draws us back to the idea of a conspiracy. Little weight is given by instrumentalists to the competition and rivalry between capitalists (as evidenced in the recent circulation 'wars' using gimmicks like bingo). Also, because power is seen as a question of personal influence, the pressure of the economic system upon the decisions that are taken is not adequately understood. Structuralists argue that we need to show how concentration and conglomeration in the newspaper industry came about if we are to explain why we have the press we do and account for its deficiencies.

The structuralist approach has been pioneered by Graham Murdock himself, in collaboration with Peter Golding. Murdock argues that 'proprietors and other capitalists do not need to intervene in newspaper production since the logic of the prevailing market structure ensures that by and large the output endorses rather than opposes their general interests' (Murdock, 1980, p. 57). If we look at the conditions under which a newspaper can make a profit it becomes clear that in order to survive it either has to attract a very large readership or a small but more affluent one. The fierceness of competition has reduced the number of titles available to consumers, and with this there has been a narrowing of the range of editorial opinion on offer, most papers identifying with the political centre or right of centre. The cut-throat economics of the business has also meant that the cost of entry into the newspaper world is now prohibitively high. For example, a plan commissioned by the TUC setting out the feasibility of starting a tabloid Labour paper estimated that it would cost some £7.7 million (*Guardian* 18.6.83). Some commentators have suggested that the situation has been worsened by the rise of the human-interest story in mass circulation papers which has led to a decline in public-affairs reporting. In order to explore the structuralist perspective in more detail, the next section will examine the growth of human-interest journalism.

The Sociology of the Human-Interest Story

James Curran, Angus Douglas and Garry Whannel have tried to trace the origins and appeal of this kind of writing. As they point out 'mass circulation papers dominate the market and contain very little about home and international news in the traditional meaning of the word *news*' (Curran, Douglas and Whannel, 1980, p. 305). They try to show how this came about.

The future of the newspaper business was in a sense decided by the industralisation it underwent in the second half of the nineteenth century. From that period on, the fixed costs of machinery and raw materials began to rise steeply as a result of technological innovation. By the 1920s the pattern was set and has continued down to the present day, interrupted only by the Second World War with its rationing of newsprint. Because of the high cost of producing the first copy, most publishers could only achieve economies of scale by pushing up the circulation of their papers. Those who failed to do this fell victim to an increase in costs and were forced to fold. Thus between 1921 and 1939 eight national newspapers closed down. At the same time the growth of advertising during this period allowed newspapers to sell at prices well below what they cost to produce, subsidising their readership through advertising revenue.

Curran *et al* illustrate the impact of these factors by the case of the re-vamping of the *Daily Mirror* between 1933–36 which turned it into a pathbreaking new enterprise at a time when it faced closure. The paper re-oriented itself to address as wide an audience as it could, bringing in new groups of readers for which advertisers were searching. One such group, according to journalist Hugh Cudlipp, consisted of 'working girls, hundreds of thousands of them working over typewriters and ledgers' who had previously read romantic fiction rather than news-papers (quoted, p. 292).

The long-term result of these market pressures has been the polarisa-tion of the press that we are familiar with today. Those papers which follow the pattern established by the *Daily Mirror* depend upon reaching a very large readership in order to remain economically viable. By contrast, 'quality' papers like *The Times* rely far more upon advertising revenue and seek to secure a small prosperous audience for upmarket advertisers – in fact, increasing their circulation may actually drive this advertising revenue away. Advertisers' satisfaction with the audience that is being delivered by a particular newspaper is crucial. Thus the *Daily Herald* closed in 1964 with a readership over five times as large as that of *The Times*, but consisting of people advertisers did not wish to reach: namely, older, male members of the working class whose purchasing power was low.

For those newspapers seeking to attract the maximum number of readers there is a need to concentrate upon those stories which represent a common denominator amongst their target audiences. As Curran *et al* point out, the evidence provided by investigations into readers' preferences have consistently shown over the last fifty years that human-interest stories 'cross the barriers of sex, class, and age, appealing almost equally to all types of reader' (p. 301). This is true for readers of quality and popular papers alike. However, the economic pressures on quality papers to maintain a small but élite audience has ensured that they have continued to deal in news. Mass circulation papers, on the other hand, have been increasingly driven to jettison this in favour of human-interest stories, a process intensified by the changes in style initiated by the *Sun* in the late sixties.

Human-interest stories are not 'news' in the traditional sense at all, because they lack any social or political context. Curran *et al* argue that they portray instead a world composed of individuals whose lives are 'strongly governed by luck, fate, and chance' and who are united in 'a community that shares common universal experiences: birth, love, death, accident, illness, and, crucially, the experience of consuming' (p. 306). Thus a typical headline would be 'MYSTERY VIRUS KILLS BOY, 3' or 'DEATH ENDS A LOVE STORY'. Indeed, the fatalistic view of life as a kind of lottery fits well with the popular papers' compulsive use of competitions, which simultaneously celebrate the virtues of conspicuous consumption in their glamorous prizes. Because their dramas are always presented in highly personal terms, the human-interest story exploits the minor doings of stars and celebrities to the full. A whole column can be written around 'the fascination David Steel has for pop stars' and his friendship with Rod Stewart. Curran *et al* argue that this type of journalism 'embodies a particular way of seeing the world', a cultural effect which is profoundly ideological in that it disguises the social and political forces that influence the shape of events (p. 306).

This study provides evidence which supports the structuralist perspective on the influence of the press. It shows that the human interest story spread because it was a formula by which newspapers could maximise the size of their readership. Although this formula tends to ignore the diversity of political beliefs amongst these readers and even to de-emphasise politics altogether, it was not introduced by capitalist proprietors as a deliberate ploy to spread ideological views but grew out of the economic necessity of reaching as big a circulation as possible.

The Problem of Choice

So far we have taken the British press as a case study of the consequences of concentration and conglomeration for the media. But how typical is the press? Do economic pressures result in restricted choice and standardised products elsewhere in the media?

The answer to this question is complex because of the differences between one medium and another. By way of a contrast, consider the case of publishing in Britain. Here, although there is free competition between firms, books are not treated like any other commodity. For one thing book prices are controlled by law. You cannot go to a big retailer like W. H. Smith to buy the latest Penguin paperback at a cheaper price in the same way that you might buy foodstuffs more cheaply at a supermarket. Also, the number of new titles published each year has continued to rise – although works of fiction as a proportion of these have tended to decline steadily since 1945, particularly novels by new authors. Fiction is however, still the largest and most popular category of book published, and in 1983 its numbers increased by 50%. It is therefore debatable whether choice has been narrowed in publishing, and media tie-ins have given quality novels like Evelyn Waugh's *Brideshead Revisited* a wider readership than they have ever enjoyed before. Nevertheless, publishing companies have been subject to mergers and takeovers in much the same way as other parts of the media and this has resulted in increased control by accountants and a greater concern with profitability and salesmanship (Lane, 1980, pp. 52–6).

Media Work and Media Organisation

The research discussed above chronicles some of the key changes in the way that the media are structured and run, and tries to show how this has affected their output. Though valuable, what these studies fail to provide is an analysis of the kind of work which goes on within the media, and the conditions under which this is carried out. This is essential if we are to have a full understanding of the factors which shape media content. We begin with some studies which look at the production of news.

News Gatekeepers

An early and influential way of looking at how potential news items come to be included in broadcasts or news pages is in terms of 'gate-keeping', a simple metaphor in which the editor is likened to a farmer standing by a gate letting some animals in and keeping others out. So, certain items are chosen while others are rejected. This idea attempts to describe some important aspects of journalistic work. The very organisation of the news room of a national daily paper is said to show the gatekeeper process in action. The news-desk receives news stories or copy and gives out the reporters' assignments each day. Once a story has been handed in it will be passed to a 'copytaster' who takes the initial decision as to whether to accept the item and forward it to a deputy editor who will give it a first title and then pass it on to be sub-edited to the required number of words. It will also be processed by specialists who look after lay-out, photographs, headlines or feature pages.

There are several criticisms of this model. Firstly, it sees news as the outcome of decisions made by individuals, notably editors, and pays scant attention to the social constraints upon journalists which stem from their sources of news. Secondly, news is seen as relatively un-problematic – it appears to be already awaiting collection, rather than having to be actively constructed or produced. As Herbert Gans has observed, 'gatekeeper theory is more easily applied to media which depend largely on wire-service news than those which also search out their own news' (Gans, 1980, p. 341).

The Routine of Newswork

The popular image of newsgathering makes it out to be an exciting business, full of drama and action, in which no one can quite be sure what is going to happen next. Dedicated to the relentless pursuit of 'hard facts', the typical news reporter is pictured as an investigator or sleuth tracking down the truth in search of the ultimate scoop.

In contrast to this rather glamorous picture, however, news is produced in bureaucratic settings which have clear hierarchies of authority and formal rules, and this has a decisive influence on the character of news. Journalists do not just search randomly for their news stories or wait for stories to break, but follow well-trodden paths and procedures laid down by the organisations to which they belong. An example of this is the 'news diary' which gives the dates of important regular announcements like the monthly unemployment figures or forthcoming visits by politicians. Journalists, in common with members of other occupations, want to be able to control their work and make it as manageable as possible and this means planning ahead. This is not to say that journalists are never faced with the sudden and the unexpected, but it does mean that a large part of the job involves the routine processing of information or stories whose general outlines are known well in advance, even it their exact details are not.

In his study of the BBC, *Putting 'Reality' Together* (1978), Philip Schlesinger points out that about 70% of the news diary is used in news bulletins so that 'most news is not spontaneous, or unanticipated' (p. 69). News is run on a daily cycle called a 'newsday' which is controlled by editorial conferences at the beginning of each cycle. These decide on how to allocate staff and resources to meet the expected flow of items for a particular day. Deadlines play a key role in organising the time of news staff and this is so marked that Schlesinger calls the TV journalists' world a 'stop-watch culture'. This obsession with time is built into the composition of the news bulletin itself, in which every picture or sentence has to be precisely timed. The bulletin is constructed around the idea of 'pace', the need (as one broadcaster put it) 'to keep the interest moving' (p. 103). This will affect the placing of individual items; stories using film, for instance, are spaced out in television news so as to guarantee variety. The requirement of pace will mean that stories will often be cut, not in order to make way for something more important, but to accommodate something shorter. Film will be used according to its availability rather than its intrinsic merit. For example, film of the assassination of the Egyptian President Anwar Sadat was very prominently featured even though it was so jumbled and chaotic that it was very hard to tell what was happening. Schlesinger also emphasises the extent to which the media is a rather closed and self-pre-occupied world. Thus the BBC makes great use of the press as a source of news items or opinion. Fishman (1978), in a study of crime reporting in New York, has suggested that this kind of mutual dependence between the different branches of the media can be an important factor in producing and sustaining exaggerated accounts of crime waves which often bear little relation to police statistics. He claims that a more accurate term would be 'media waves'.

News Values and Professional Ideologies

Like any other specialised occupation, journalism has its own beliefs and values. These provide guidelines for carrying out journalistic work and a self-image which justifies the profession as a whole. Several writers have argued that these factors are important in determining what is presented as news, as well as the form it takes.

A good example of this type of approach is the study of what have come to be known as *news values*. Galtung and Ruge (1965) in their analysis of foreign news reporting see news values as falling into two broad types: bureaucratic and cultural. Bureaucratic values are closely tied to the routine of the job and the nature of the final product. For example, in order to qualify as news an item must have a timespan that fits in with the work schedule of the medium in question. A newspaper, like TV, operates on a 24 hour cycle and will prefer stories that follow this same rhythm – thus the building of a dam would be ignored, but its public opening would not be. Also, newspapers have to fill fixed amounts of space or time allocated to different types of story (e.g. crime, foreign news, sport) irrespective of how much news is actually happening in the real world. News also tends to be based on certain cultural values: particular attention will be paid to 'the familiar, to the culturally similar, and the culturally distant will be passed by more easily and not be noticed' (Galtung and Ruge, 1965, p. 67). Thus there is a legendary journalist's rule of thumb known as 'McLurg's Law' which states that air crashes or other major accidents in Asia should normally get less coverage than those in Europe. Galtung and Ruge also mention other typical news values: these include reference to members of élites, the reporting of events in terms of personalities, and a preference for negative news.

Values like these help buttress journalists' claims to be professionals, to be 'as unequivocally recognised as members of a skilled and learned profession as those who follow medicine and law' (Christian, 1980, p. 290). As well as making a case for higher pay and higher status, this is also a claim that journalists should be given a maximum of independence in order to do their job properly. Jock Young (1981) has suggested that this self-justifying professional ideology grows out of the journalist's unique position in the production of news. Firstly, they are situated between production workers on the one side and management on the other, distanced from the main lines of conflict in industry. Secondly, the job itself involves a high degree of individual responsibility for the work that is carried out; its standards are meritocratic and individualistic. Thirdly, the variability in the work of producing news stories is unusual compared to most other jobs, and helps generate a special sense of professional identity. As Young notes, 'the only parallel to a news journalist would be if the designers in Fords made a new model car every day' (p. 418).

Part of this professional ideology is a view of what the audience wants and how to supply it. Philip Schlesinger has observed that 'newsmen do not doubt that they know what is wanted' and 'they explain their knowledge by invoking the related notions of professionalism, commitment, and experience' (1978, p. 116). Thus, although television ratings are routinely monitored, these are relatively uninformative and journalists largely rely upon their own 'news sense' rather than audience response when deciding on programme content. This may sometimes go awry – as one BBC man told Schlesinger: 'In the end it's professional judgement and we're not always right' (p. 120). As we saw in the last section, their professional judgement is reinforced by an intense awareness of what is being produced by other news media. The professional culture of journalists makes it an imperative for them to immerse themselves in news, and their work ethic requires that the good journalist keeps up with what is happening even while on holiday.

Objectivity in Practice: A Strategic Ritual

We have already seen that objectivity is one of the ideal standards of journalism. In an important article Gaye Tuchman (1972) examined the work routines of journalists on a daily city newspaper in the United States to see how they made use of it in their everyday professional lives. She studied the paper as a participant observer, following its daily round unobtrusively. Her findings suggest that while objective reporting may be an ideal, in practice it refers to a set of procedures which are used by journalists to avoid unnecessary trouble.

Tuchman argues that the norms defining objectivity are best understood as guidelines for reducing the risks of the job. Reporters have to cope with a number of pressures which could undermine their professional credibility. All journalists have to meet the demand that they adhere to daily deadlines and failure to do so can have disastrous results: the printing of the paper may be delayed, its distribution held up allowing drivers to claim overtime payments for working late, and the postponed delivery may mean that customers choose to buy a rival newspaper resulting in a squeeze on profits. At the same time, reporters have to keep an eye open for editorial criticism of the accuracy of their stories, and must always beware of leaving themselves open to be sued for libel or misrepresentation. Unfortunately, speed and accuracy are not easily reconciled demands. In the time available to gather together the basics of a good story, reporters are forced to take many items of information on trust. Although they are required to check their facts this cannot always be done. It would be impractical if they were to indicate every single unexamined statement in their stories, and it would make stilted reading. There are limits to how many questions the reporter can ask and still meet the afternoon deadline. But in order to make themselves less vulnerable they adopt a set of safeguards which allow them to claim that they really are being objective.

Tuchman argues that journalists resort to what she calls 'strategic rituals'. These are very similar to those found in pre-industrial societies: as she observes, 'newspapermen invoke their objectivity almost the way a Mediterranean peasant might wear a clove of garlic around his neck to ward off evil spirits' (p. 660). In other words, reporters have a number of tricks of the trade which allow them to hold editorial criticism at bay, even though these merely avoid the real problems of objectivity rather than solve them. Such rituals can be considered 'strategic' because they act as a means of self-defence, a symbolic way of side-stepping future censure or attack.

There are several different forms that strategic rituals can take. First of all, journalists may find themselves in a situation in which it is hard to tell that which an informant is saying is correct or not. For example, a claim by a Democratic Party senator that America is lagging behind the Soviet Union in nuclear weaponry would be difficult for a reporter to check. A way out of the difficulty is for the reporter to search out an alternative point of view – he or she could contact the Secretary of Defence from the opposing Republican Party for instance – and then set down the two contrasting statements side by side. Without trying to assess who is right, the reporter simply prints both statements and needs make no further attempt to find out the truth. This 'presentation of conflicting possibilities' gives the reporter the best of both worlds – a set of 'facts' have been revealed and the editorial deadline has been met. Yet the truth of the matter is left undecided and un-investigated.

Another strategic ritual is the 'presentation of supporting evidence'. This involves the piling of fact upon fact in such a way as to *appear* to shed light on a topic, when strictly speaking no firm conclusions may be drawn. Tuchman gives the example of an obituary in the newspaper she studied in which a reporter referred to the deceased as a 'master musician'. When the editor questioned this he was told that the musician had once played with a famous composer, and this additional information was enough to satisfy the editor that the reporter had covered himself. Here, once again, we have something less than complete objectivity – an objective statement is implied but never really justified or proved.

A final ritual safeguard relies on the 'judicious use of quotation marks' as a way of avoiding charges of inaccuracy and bias. Tuchman cites the case of a reporter covering an anti-Vietnam War rally. Privately the reporter was very impressed by the demonstration and supported its aims, but knew that to say this would be to bring censure from unsympathetic editors. The reporter therefore wrote a column whose tone was favourable to the demonstrators, but which carefully used quotation marks in order to distance himself from what was being said. A typical sentence ran: 'some thousands of persons swarmed to a sunny City Park yesterday to an "incredibly successful" anti-draft, anti-war rally' (p. 669). Here the quotation marks are a way of saying that the words in question do not belong to the reporter. Carefully used they create an impression which colours our understanding of events, while still allowing the journalist to claim to be unbiased. Tuchman's study shows how these taken-for-granted procedures underpin journalists' conventional judgments as to what counts as news and how it is to be presented.

News as Commercial Knowledge: The Work of the Crime Reporter

In another study of journalists at work based on a series of interviews with crime reporters, Steve Chibnall (1975) has produced an important critique of the gatekeeper approach. His research suggests that instead of being determined by editorial selection, what will be in the news will have already been decided upon long before the reporter's copy has reached the editor's desk.

Crime reporters are highly specialised and rely almost exclusively upon a single source of information. Of the seventy Fleet Street journalists who regularly report on crime only about one-third are full-time crime reporters. Chibnall argues that these are really 'police reporters'. Orginally a crime reporter was merely someone who went round the London police stations in search of tit-bits of information which could be passed on to senior journalists. However, as crime stories gained in importance a Scotland Yard Press Bureau was founded in the mid-1920s to provide official statements to the growing body of crime reporters, making them a more specialised professional group than they previously were.

However, one of the problems with this Press Bureau was that it failed to meet these journalists' needs. The press officers were seen as a kind of barrier between reporters and senior policemen and often the information which was released came too late to be used by the press.

Furthermore, press releases were, by definition, given out to *all* reporters and this hindered the compiling of an exclusive news story. Reporters even doubted whether press officers could really recognise a good story. The local representatives of the bureau, the Divisional Liaison Officers or DLOs, were nicknamed the 'Don't Let Ons' by the press because of the way in which they were felt to withhold information.

Difficulties of this kind have led crime reporters to carefully cultivate close personal contacts with police officers as an alternative source of news. Status in this field of work depends upon both the number and quality of contacts at a reporter's disposal. In fact, if it is justifiable to talk about gatekeepers in crime reporting at all, those gatekeepers are the police. Ultimately the police have a strong veto power over the reporter who would be out of a job if this supply of information dried up. However, despite this asymmetry between the two parties, these relationships have a certain equality about them because both sides have something to offer. Although reporters rarely give the police cash payments, such sources may be expensive where money is lavishly spent on food and drink in order to create a sociable atmosphere for exchanging information. Most of the information received is 'paid for' by the return of favours. There are two kinds of service that the press can give. Firstly, reporters can anonymously pass on tip-offs from their criminal contacts which could not be given directly to the police for fear of incrimination. More generally, an important resource that reporters have is their discretion in handling information. The press can be used by the police as a means of appealing to the public for help, and can also take a direct part in police operations by releasing information which is deliberately misleading – for example, by 'declaring that bank raiders have stolen a million rather than half a million pounds, in the hopes of causing the thieves to fall out' (p. 56). The press can also give 'promotional aid', since crime reporters do not just deal with crime, but write on police pay and conditions and police politics. Providing a sympathetic view of police work and police causes is therefore one of the most important bargaining points that the reporter has, though it is usually part of an unspoken agreement.

Chibnall sees the reporter's news story as a product – knowledge which is bought and sold. As one journalist told him: 'I regard news as a commodity – it's there to buy, it's there to report' (p. 59). In transforming his or her material into a marketable form, the journalist is involved in the work of packaging. This is not merely a response to reader demand but is constrained by a number of other factors. First of all, crime reporters have their own specialised version of journalistic news values which give priority to some stories over others. For example, they tend to ignore certain crimes altogether. 'Company fraud is a difficult thing to write about', said one reporter in interview, 'you can't work clichés into it, there's no violence, no drama' (p. 58). Secondly, reporters are constrained by their relations with their sources. For example, a story may be held back at a sensitive moment in a police investigation. There may also be a tendency to turn a blind eye to police misdemeanours for fear of losing one's source. At times, therefore, 'the informal ethics of police work dominate the formal ethics of journalism' (p. 61).

In explaining the characteristics of news, Chibnall (1977) takes issue with Marxian approaches, which he suggests are unclear about how economic interests actually determine what appears in the press. He attacks the Marxist writer Ralph Miliband's contention that the capitalist ideology of the owners and controllers of the press is passed down to editors and journalists, limiting the range of ideas and views they express, since it tells us little about how the 'seeping downwards' of ideology happens. We should not see journalists as 'simply puppets on strings pulled by capitalists' as some instrumentalist or conspiracy theorists propose (1977, p. 224). Chibnall argues that we need instead to focus upon the day to day situation of reporters in order to understand what they write. Journalists have to negotiate the demands of four sets of people – editors, colleagues, sources and readers – all of whom have to be satisfied. Although news is 'commercial knowledge', a special kind of knowledge which has to be sold to the public, it is brought into being under a variety of constraints. None of these can be reduced to a single economic factor as writers on ownership and control in the media argue. For Chibnall 'police sources exert a more immediate influence on crime reporters' accounts than do newspaper proprietors or even, perhaps, the economic conditions of newspaper production' (p. 225). Even where they are dependent upon a single source, reporters bargain and exchange information and services, and exercise choice within the social limits that their job imposes using the received professional wisdom of their craft.

Cultural Industries and the Problem of Fads and Fashions

Other branches of the media also develop complex professional strategies in order to cope with the uncertainties of their work. Paul Hirsch's (1972) comparative analysis of American commercial publishing houses, film studios and record companies looks at the problems faced by those in the business of supplying a product that is meant to be creatively or expressively unique. If, for example, a film simply repeated other films, it would fail to find a market. At the same time, because they are operating for commercial rather than purely aesthetic motives, these cultural industries need to standardise production and distribution as much as possible in order to maximise their profits.

Although it is possible to reduce the risks involved by resorting to tried and trusted formulas or employing famous stars, no-one can be absolutely sure what will guarantee a best-seller. Cultural industries are always seeking to capitalise on fads and fashions, but these are by their very nature unpredictable. To get round this difficulty, companies have to rely upon the professional judgement of specialist personnel who operate on the peripheries of the organisation and whose work cuts across technical, artistic and managerial responsibilities. They include talent scouts, acquisitions editors, record producers and film directors, as well as promoters, press coordinators, and public relations staff. Hirsch refers to these as 'boundary-spanning roles': they link the organisation to new sources of talent and keep it in touch with potential audiences. Not only are they accorded a great deal of professional autonomy, but 'their value to the cultural organisation as recruiters and intelligence agents is indicated by high salaries, commissions, and prestige within the industry system' (p. 651).

Secondly, these industries try to deal with the uncertainty of their markets by overproducing; thus 'the number of books, records and low-budget films released annually far exceeds coverage capacity and consumer demand for these products' (p. 652). This is a way for companies to hedge their bets. The point here is that a wide spread of products will ensure that at least *some* are successful, and this is less costly than only promoting a few items which have been expensively market-researched. Finally, Hirsch notes that cultural industries need to obtain coverage by the other mass media to ensure the successful promotion of their products. Disc jockeys, book critics and film reviewers all act as 'surrogate consumers' by giving the public a guide to what is on offer. They can effectively regulate the access a producer has to an audience by influencing popular taste and buying habits. Although surrogate consumers have to be seen to safeguard their independence of judgement if they are to retain credibility with their audiences, cultural industries will seek to co-opt them. This has always been a sensitive area and one that has sometimes led to conflict. The most famous instances are the notorious American 'payola' scandals of the 1950s in which there was a public outcry against the major record companies for paying off disc jockeys as an incentive to play their new releases. In fact this practice was only officially made illegal in 1960.

The Media and Technological Change

Hirsch's concept of 'cultural industries' serves as a timely reminder that the mass media are first and foremost work organisations and depend upon the labour of technicians, engineers and workers at a variety of levels of skill. This tends to be submerged below the exciting image the media projects of itself as a world of stars, personalities and glamorous professionals. The technology underpinning the mass media has been constantly changing throughout this century, and probably never more rapidly that at present. We conclude with a comparison of two very different kinds of work within the media which have been radically altered as a result of changes in technology: the sound mixer and the printer.

The technology of sound mixing in the record industry has tended to become progressively more sophisticated since the 1940s. In the early days the recording technician's skill involved placing and balancing microphones and making best use of the acoustics of the studio in an endeavour to reproduce the sound of the concert hall. In America these studios were large and capital-intensive and this led to craft union organisation amongst these workers. This system was undermined in the early fifties by the development of tape recording which simplified studio technology and considerably lowered its cost. It became easy to set up small studios to produce records for the minority-taste audiences which the radio industry was trying to reach as it began to reorganise itself after losing its mass audience to television. These were the days of the rise of rock 'n' roll, and sound mixers began to work in small entrepreneur-run settings developing new recording skills based on echo and reverberation equipment. In the 1960s the technology of recording became considerably more complex with the advent of multi-tracking. Rock musicians themselves began to challenge the sound mixer's prerogative of control over the technical details of recording and would insist on mixing their own tapes personally. Edward Kealy (1979) has noted that this has led to a new type of studio professional which he terms the 'artist-mixer', who was often an ex-rock musician and shared in the artistic ambitions of the rock groups. Such figures free-lance and compete for bonuses and royalties, and are now awarded Gold Records by record companies for outstanding commercial success in the same way that recording artists are. Kealy argues that the evolution of this type of work is 'a counter-example to the general trend in the development of the modern work experience' which is towards routinisation and de-skilling (p. 26).

Cynthia Cockburn's book about changes in the British newspaper printing industry, *Brothers* (1983), tells a different story. Although printers' immediate influence on the content of newspapers has typically been limited to the very occasional veto on material viewed as anti-union, they have had a major impact upon the structure and organisation of the press as a whole. Now, however, the traditional technology of linotype machines, hand assembled pages and rotary letterpress printing is gradually being replaced by computer-assisted techniques of photo-composition in which newspaper copy is typed directly into a computer and printed out ready for use. Eventually whole pages could be assembled on a computer screen and then transformed by a digital typesetter into printable output. The effect of these changes upon the workforce have been twofold. On the one hand, the new technology has meant increased earnings, shorter working hours and an improved working environment without the noise, grime and sheer physical effort of the old crafts. On the other, the skills which the new technology requires are far less specific than those they are replacing, and are increasingly being found throughout industry wherever computers are introduced. Thus the scarcity value of the printer is being eroded in a period of rising unemployment and the hand of the owners has been strengthened.

Although few of the workers whom Cockburn interviewed wanted to return to the old conditions, most of them felt that something had been lost. As one said: 'I think I have gone from skilled to semi-skilled, that's what it is. And I feel a bit let down. It has been a worry in my mind all the time' (p. 118). Cockburn stresses that one important dimension of this process is the undermining of the implicitly patriarchal nature of the craft. Women have always been a more excluded or marginalised group in newspaper printing than in other branches of the trade, and men have disproportionately benefitted from this discrimination. As Cockburn comments: 'in the last resort, the craft work of composition for print was men's work *because men said it was*', and they maintained this position by actively campaigning against women (p. 152). Ironically, part of the effect of the new technology is to bring printworkers' jobs closer to the office work that has traditionally been seen as women's work, and this is very threatening to them. 'If *girls* can do it, you know, then you are sort of deskilled you know, really', commented one male printworker (p. 118).

82069

Cockburn shows that skill is about gender as much it is about social class, since it is partly defined by ideologies of masculinity. Whether the position of women will be changed in the new large-scale union amalgamations, NGA-82 and SOGAT-82, which have been the printworkers' major response to the new technology remains to be seen.

The present is viewed as a watershed by some writers who see industrial societies as poised to take off into a novel and unprecedented phase, perhaps an era of *post-industralism* based upon the new information technology, the combination of telecommunications with the microchip. Similarly, the introduction of satellite and cable technology has led to predictions that the mass media will completely re-shape day to day life in the near future. Once familiar media may decline dramatically or even disappear altogether under the impact of new technological and cultural forms. Cinema, for example, 'could well end up confined to the larger city centres (especially London) and a small fringe of cinephiles by the mid-'80s' (Blanchard, 1983, p. 109). Whatever the future holds we can expect that it will not only raise new problems but also, as the story of the mass media to date has shown, it will re-kindle old criticisms from the past.

Bibliography

Abercrombie, N., Hill, S., and Turner, B.S. *The Dominant Ideology Thesis* (George Allen & Unwin, London, 1980)

Adams, C. and Laurikietis, R. *The Gender Trap, Book 3: Messages and Images* (Virago, London, 1976)

Belson, W. *Television Violence and the Adolescent Boy* (Saxon House, Farnborough, 1978)

Bennett, T. 'Text and Social Process: The Case of James Bond' *Screen Education* no 41, Winter/Spring 1982a

Bennett, T. 'Media, "reality", signification' in M. Gurevitch *et al*, 1982b

Blanchard, S. 'Cinema-Going, Going, Gone?' *Screen* vol 24 nos 4–5, July–Oct. 1983

Boorstin, D. *The Image* (Penguin Books, Harmondsworth, 1962)

Braham, P. 'How the Media Report Race' in M. Gurevitch *et al*, 1982

Cantril, H. *The Invasion from Mars: a Study in the Psychology of Panic* (Princeton University Press, Princeton, 1940)

Chibnall, S. 'The Crime Reporter: A Study in the Production of Commercial Knowledge' *Sociology* vol 9, 1975

Chibnall, S. *Law-and-Order News: an Analysis of Crime Reporting in the British Press* (Tavistock London, 1977)

Christian, H. 'Journalists' Occupational Ideologies and Press Commercialisation' in *The Sociology of Journalism and the Press* edited by H. Christian (Sociological Review Monograph 29, University of Keele, Oct. 1980)

Cockburn, C. *Brothers: Male Dominance and Technological Change* (Pluto Press, London, 1983)

Cohen, S. *Folk Devils and Moral Panics: the Creation of the Mods and Rockers* (Mac-Gibbon & Kee, London, 1972)

Cohen, S. and Young, J. *The Manufacture of News: Deviance, Social Problems and the Mass Media* (Constable, London, 1981)

Collins, H. *Marxism and Law* (Oxford University Press, Oxford, 1982)

Cook, J. and Lewington, M. (eds) *Images of Alcoholism* (British Film Institute, London, 1979)

Curran, J., Gurevitch, M. and Woollacott, J. (eds) *Mass Communication and Society* (Edward Arnold, London, 1977)

Curran, J., Douglas, A. and Whannel, G. 'The Political Economy of the Human-Interest Story' in *Newspapers and Democracy: International Essays on a Changing Medium* edited by A. Smith (Massachusetts Institute of Technology Press, Cambridge, Mass., 1980)

Ditton, J. and Duffy, J. 'Bias in the Newspaper Reporting of Crime News' *British Journal of Criminology* vol 23 no 2, April 1983

Durkheim, E. *Suicide: A Study in Sociology* (Routledge & Kegan Paul, London, 1952)

Elliott, P. 'Review of *More Bad News* by the Glasgow University Media Group' *Sociological Review* vol 29 no I, Feb. 1981)

Eysenck, H.J. and Nias, D.K.B. *Sex, Violence and the Media* (Paladin, London, 1980)

Ferguson, M. *Forever Feminine: Women's Magazines and the Cult of Femininity* (Heinemann, London, 1983)

Fishman, M. 'Crime Waves as Ideology' *Social Problems* vol 25 no 4, June 1978

Fowler, B. ' "True To Me Always": An Analysis of Women's Magazine Fiction' *British Journal of Sociology* vol 30 no I, March 1979

Frith, S. *Sound Effects: Youth, Leisure and the Politics of Rock 'n' Roll* (Constable, London, 1983)

Gans, H.J. *Deciding What's News: a Study of CBS Evening News, NBC Nightly News, Newsweek and Time* (Constable, London, 1980)

Galtung, J. and Ruge, M.H. 'The Structure of Foreign News' *Journal of Peace Research* vol 2, 1965

Gitlin, T. 'Media Sociology: the Dominant Paradigm' *Theory and Society* vol 6 no 2, Sept. 1978

Glasgow University Media Group *Bad News* (Routledge & Kegan Paul, London, 1976)

Glasgow University Media Group *More Bad News* (Routledge & Kegan Paul, London, 1980)

Glasgow University Media Group *Really Bad News* (Writers & Readers, London, 1982)

Goffman, E. *Gender Advertisements* (Macmillan, London, 1979)

Gurevitch, M., Bennett, T., Curran, J. and Woollacott, J. (eds) *Culture, Society and the Media* (Methuen, London, 1982)

Gurevitch, M. and Blumler, J. 'Linkages between the Mass Media and Politics: a Model for the Analysis of Political Communications Systems' in J. Curran *et al*, 1977

Hall, S. 'The Rediscovery of "Ideology": Return of the Repressed in Media Studies' in M. Gurevitch *et al,* 1982

Hall, S., Critcher, C., Jefferson, T., Clarke, J. and Roberts, B. *Policing the Crisis: Mugging, the State and Law and Order* (Macmillan, London, 1978)

Hartmann, P., *et al* 'Race as News' in *Race as News* edited by J. D. Halloran (UNESCO, Paris, 1974)

Hirsch, P. M. 'Processing Fads and Fashions: an Organization Set Analysis of Cultural Industry Systems' *American Journal of Sociology* vol 77 no 4, 1972

Howitt, D. *Mass Media and Social Problems* (Pergamon Press, Oxford, 1982)

Katz, E. and Lazarsfeld, P. *Personal Influence* (The Free Press, New York, 1955)

Kealy, E. 'From Craft to Art: the Case of Sound Mixers and Popular Music' *Sociology of Work and Occupations* vol 6 no I, Feb. 1979

Kuhn, T. *The Structure of Scientific Revolutions* (University of Chicago Press, Chicago, 1962)

Laing, D. 'The Music Industry in Crisis' *Marxism Today* July 1981

Lane, M. *Books and Publishers: Commerce Against Culture in Postwar Britain* (D. C. Heath & Co., Lexington, Mass., 1980)

Lea, J. and Young, J. 'Urban Violence and Political Marginalisation: The Riots in Britain; Summer 1981' *Critical Social Policy* vol I, no 3, Spring 1982

McQuail, D. (ed) *Sociology of Mass Communications* (Penguin, Harmondsworth, 1972)

McQuail, D., Blumler, J. G. and Brown, J. R. 'The Television Audience: A Revised Perspective' in McQuail, 1972

Marx, K. *Capital Vol. III* (Penguin, Harmondsworth, 1981)

Marx, K. and Engels, F. *The German Ideology* (Lawrence & Wishart, London, 1965)

Miliband, R. *The State in Capitalist Society* (Quartet Books, London, 1973)

Morley, D. *The 'Nationwide' Audience* (British Film Institute, London, 1980)

Murdock, G. and Golding, P. 'Capitalism, Communications and Class Relations' in J. Curran *et al*, 1977

Murdock, G. and McCron, R. 'The Broadcasting and Delinquency Debate' *Screen Education* no 30, Spring 1979

Murdock, G. 'Class, Power and the Press: Problems of Conceptualisation and Evidence' in H. Christian, 1980

Murdock, G. 'Large Corporations and the Control of the Communications Industries' in M. Gurevitch *et al*, 1982

Palmer, J. *Thrillers: Genesis and Structure of a Popular Genre* (Edward Arnold, London, 1979)

Plummer, K. 'Misunderstanding Labelling Perspectives' in *Deviant Interpretations* edited by D. Downes and P. Rock (Martin Robertson, Oxford, 1979)

Robins, D. and Cohen, P. 'Enter the Dragon' in Cohen and Young, 1981

Rosengren, K. E. and Windahl, S. 'Mass Media Consumption as a Functional Alternative' in McQuail, 1972

Scott, J. *Corporations, Classes and Capitalism* (Hutchinson, London, 1979)

Schlesinger, P. *Putting 'Reality' Together* (Constable, London 1978)

Tracey, M. and Morrison, D. *Whitehouse* (Macmillan, London, 1979)

Troyna, B. *Public Awareness and the Media: a Study of Reporting Race* (Commission for Racial Equality, London, 1981)

Tuchman, G. 'Objectivity as Strategic Ritual: an Examination of Newsmen's Notions of Objectivity' *American Journal of Sociology* vol 77, 1972

Tudor, A. 'On Alcohol and the Mystique of Media Effects' in J. Cook and M. Lewington, 1979

Tunstall, J. *The Media in Britain* (Constable, London, 1983)

Whale, J. *The Politics of the Media* (Fontana, London, 1977)

Williams, B. *Obscenity and Film Censorship: An Abridgement of the Williams Report* (Cambridge University Press, Cambridge, 1981)

Wolff, J. *The Social Production of Art* (Macmillan, London, 1981)

Woollacott, J. 'Teaching Them to Read: The Politics of Imagination' *Schooling and Culture* Issue 7, Spring 1980

Young, J. 'Beyond the Consensual Paradigm: A Critique of Left Functionalism in Media Theory' in S. Cohen and J. Young, 1981

Index